HEALING HAPPENS

with Your Help

Also by Carol Ritberger, Ph.D.

Books

LOVE . . . WHAT'S PERSONALITY GOT TO DO WITH IT?: Working at Love to Make Love Work

MANAGING PEOPLE . . . WHAT'S PERSONALITY GOT TO DO WITH IT?

WHAT COLOR IS YOUR PERSONALITY?
Red, Orange, Yellow, Green . . .

YOUR PERSONALITY, YOUR HEALTH:
Connecting Personality with the Human Energy System, Chakras, and Wellness

Audio Program

YOUR PERSONALITY, YOUR HEALTH, AND YOUR LIFE
(includes workbook)

HEALING HAPPENS

with Your Help

Understanding the Hidden
Meanings Behind Illness

Carol Ritberger, Ph.D.

HAY HOUSE, INC.
Carlsbad, California • New York City
London • Sydney • Johannesburg
Vancouver • Hong Kong • New Delhi

Published and distributed in the United States by: Hay House, Inc.: www.hay
house.com • *Published and distributed in Australia by:* Hay House Australia Pty.
Ltd.: www.hayhouse.com.au • *Published and distributed in the United Kingdom
by:* Hay House UK, Ltd.: www.hayhouse.co.uk • *Published and distributed in the
Republic of South Africa by:* Hay House SA (Pty), Ltd.: www.hayhouse.co.za •
Distributed in Canada by: Raincoast: www.raincoast.com • *Published in India
by:* Hay House Publishers India: www.hayhouse.co.in

Design: Tricia Breidenthal

Library of Congress Cataloging-in-Publication Data

Ritberger, Carol.
  Healing happens with your help : understanding the hidden meanings
behind illness / Carol Ritberger. -- 1st ed.
     p. cm.
  Includes bibliographical references.
  ISBN-13: 978-1-4019-1760-9 (tradepaper) 1. Healing. 2. Medicine, Psy-
chosomatic. I. Title.
  RZ999.R58 2008
  615.5'3--dc22
                                        2007030789

             ISBN: 978-1-4019-1760-9

         11 10 09 08   4 3 2 1
            1st edition, February 2008

*This book is dedicated to
our daughter Cynthia Franke
who healed herself because
she believed she could.*

CONTENTS

INTRODUCTION

Illness Isn't about the Obvious

The purpose of this book is straightforward: It's about healing and what you can do to heal yourself. However, this isn't necessarily easy, because how you engage in the process is strongly influenced by the perceptions you have.

Let me explain. If you see illness as the result of external factors such as viruses, bacterial infections, environmental contaminants, or something you ingest, then your approach to healing will be focused primarily on the needs of the body. If you view illness as a form of psychological payback for something you've done wrong, then it will be difficult for you to understand it as an opportunity to learn more about yourself, serving as a powerful catalyst to change what is causing you pain and suffering in your life. If you expect others to heal you and you buy into the treatment mentality that one size fits all, then you won't understand that illness is your individual quest for *wholeness.* Most important, if you think that it's about the obvious, then the chances of your successfully healing yourself are significantly decreased, because it isn't about what's readily apparent. Instead, it concerns the underlying factors that strongly impact every aspect of your life.

Illness is about what lies deep within the human psyche—the thoughts, emotions, attitudes, beliefs, perceptions, and core themes that influence what we think, how we feel about ourselves, why we act the way we do, our sense of reality, and whether we believe that we can heal ourselves or not. It reflects the stories of our life and discloses how conditioning has impacted our sense of self. And it doesn't just affect the body; it has an impact on the mind, the energy body, and the soul as well. In a sense, it represents a psychospiritual disconnection between these elements and brings to our attention the changes that must be made if we're to restore ourselves to good health.

Via the soul/mind/body connection, illness reveals where we're energetically storing negative emotions in our organs, glands, and muscles and where we're holding fears and beliefs in our spine. Since it involves more than meets the eye, then how we treat it must be expanded from just dealing with the needs of the body to addressing the source that's responsible for the disconnection—the mind. Without a change in mental state, the soul, the energy body, and the physical self will continue to be at the mercy of the factors that lie deep within the workings of the mind.

The Perception of Separation

Throughout the history of medicine, physicians and metaphysicians have agreed on the factors that contributed to the formation of illness. They knew that addressing it required the healing of the whole self, and that it all must begin with the mental state. So what caused the shift in perception that so radically altered the way illness was viewed, diagnosed, and treated? What caused it to move from the holistic psychospiritual view to the scientific tenet that the mind and body are separate, which chooses not to acknowledge the presence of the soul or its healing powers? This theory clearly devalues the curative powers of the soul and doesn't even deal with its needs. It doesn't take into consideration the psychological factors that are deeply buried within the illness. Why aren't these being addressed? Perhaps we can find the answers to these questions if we consider how the evolution of the consciousness of medicine has shifted to the perception of separation that:

- Places value only on what's tangible and what can be measured through double-blind studies

- Doesn't fully understand the connection between thoughts and emotions and the significant role they play in the formation of illness, specifically on the impact of the immune system

- Chooses to separate the mind from the body and these two from the soul, and has forgotten that the physical body loses its vitality when this split occurs, thus leaving it susceptible to illness

- Loses sight of the fact that healing can't occur without addressing all of the contributors responsible for the formation of illness, including thoughts, emotions, attitudes, beliefs, perceptions, and core themes

- Views the body from a biomechanical perspective that thinks its parts aren't connected,
  rather than a holistic perspective that considers the physical self a whole system

- Forgets that illness and good health are a continuum and that the difference between the
  two lies in the quality of thought

- Overlooks the purpose of illness

The Purpose of Illness

Illness basically reflects how the soul, the mind, and the
body are interacting with each other and how all three are
responding, adjusting, and adapting to both internal and
external influences. Its presence is telling us that something
in our thoughts, words, actions, and lifestyle is compromising who we are, and that's causing a disconnection in the
electrochemical communication process among the three.
Illness reveals how that rupture is compromising the body's
ability to function properly and impacting the mind's ability
to correct the problem. It's showing how the soul is struggling to reestablish an open line of communication.

The purpose of illness is to alert us that change is
required if we're to experience good health. It's telling us
that we need to alter the negative thoughts responsible for
creating the limitations that hold us back and distort how
we see ourselves. It brings attention to the fact that those
thoughts are creating detrimental attitudes, which are leading to abnormal behavior. There can be no more replaying
of the harsh internal talk or rehashing the same old stories

responsible for our emotional hurts. It tells us that we must cease berating ourselves because we didn't do what we thought we should or could.

Illness can tell us that we need to change our lifestyle if it isn't conducive to good health and modify unhealthy habits that are impacting the well-being of the body. It can reveal that perhaps we should reevaluate the kinds of interactions we're attracting or tell us it's time to get out of an emotionally destructive relationship. It can relay that we need to start expressing our emotions rather than suppressing them, because doing so is affecting our immunity.

Whenever illness comes calling—be it in the form of muscle tension, aches, pains, or other diagnosable signs—it's telling us clearly and succinctly that we'd better change what's causing the disconnection between the soul, mind, and body because it's beginning to do harm.

Another purpose of illness is to heighten our mental awareness of physical needs and to focus our attention—sometimes to the point of being overly preoccupied—on what's happening in the mind/body connection. This heightened state can sometimes create anxiousness or restlessness, and the objective behind such behavior is to alert the mind that it needs to listen to the messages of the body and not continue to ignore them.

As an example, let's use the situation of an irregular heartbeat that's been occurring for some time. Since heart rhythms affect overall physical performance, the body has been sending out little warning messages alerting the mind that there may be a problem and that it needs to slow down enough to notice that every time we get stressed, our heartbeat becomes irregular. It's as if the body has been whispering to the mind that something's awry and that it needs to create a response that will encourage us to have things checked out.

However when we're under strain, such messages go unrecognized because we're usually so much in our heads that we forget we even have a physical self. In this case, the body increases the volume of its communication until the mind must deal with it because we're experiencing the stress response of fight-or-flight. At this point, the body has the mind's attention because it can't think clearly. It becomes alarmed because the heart is racing, breathing is rapid and shallow, and it felt the heart skip a beat. The mind is now so focused on the irregular heartbeats that it immediately creates thoughts telling us that we need to have it checked out and monitored by a doctor.

The risk that comes from the body having to go to these kinds of extreme measures to be heard is that it takes a lot of energy, it adds wear and tear on the physical structure, and it breaks down the immune system's protective ability. Over the course of time, such measures can lead to serious health problems.

What Illness Is About

Illness is about the quality of our thoughts because they're what determine who we are, what we become, how we feel, and the state of our health and well-being. Everything we say and do; how we act and interact with other people; and every situation, event, and experience we attract are all a reflection of what we're thinking. In the case of illness, the thoughts being created are counterproductive to the needs of the soul and body and are causing both to be compromised to the point of becoming ill. They're putting us in a protective mode versus a growth mode. When in such a condition, the vital energy of the soul and energy body is depleted, and the physical self is put in a state of hormonal crisis. This increases blood pressure and acidity in the digestive tract and can lead to glandular problems such as hypothyroidism, hyperthyroidism, adrenal disorders, pancreatitis, and reproductive issues. It also forces the mind to remain in a hypervigilant state of mental arousal, which can cause psychological fatigue and lead to anxiety disorders and insomnia.

Unfortunately, many of the thoughts that drive our behavior and influence the choices we make are more reflective of our conditioning and other people's perceptions and opinions than our own. When this is the case, there's a tendency to find ourselves stuck in old thinking patterns and constrained by the same mental limitations as adults that we did as children. It seems that early training has such a powerful hold that we can spend most of our adult lives trying to free ourselves from it. Consequently, it's sometimes easier to take the path of least resistance and stick with what's familiar and tried-and-true than it is to change. As a result, we develop what I call the "Been There, Done That Syndrome" which eventually increases our susceptibility to becoming unwell.

Illness is also about lifestyles, habits, and patterns of behavior. As we become busier and the demands on our time more urgent, we're creating expectations and engaging in activities that leave very little time for relaxation or rebuilding health. We're eating on the run and choosing the wrong foods, we're resting less and using sleep aids to try to get a few hours a night, and we're taking antidepressants and tranquilizers at an alarming rate. (Americans are consuming over 1.5 million pounds of these drugs annually.)

Our thoughts are consumed with staying thin and trying any diet program that comes along and promises to drop those stress-related pounds. Alcoholism and drug use are on the rise even though we know they shorten life expectancy. So is smoking, despite our knowledge that the habit will cause lung cancer. People continue to light up even though they know it's bad for them, and do so even when they can't cross a room without running out of breath. Why? Because trying to kick the habit is so unpleasant that it's easier to stay with it than it is to change. Unfortunately, while we know it's harmful to the body, the brain becomes so addicted that it relies on these chemicals as a coping mechanism to help deal with the demands of the outer world. Consequently, the brain creates thoughts supporting the habit.

Current research in the field of psychoneuroimmunology, the study of the relationship between emotions and the functioning of the immune system, reveals that patterns of behavior also play a significant role in increasing susceptibility to illness, specifically to diagnoses such as cardiovascular disease, asthma, depression, autoimmune disorders, and cancer. The scientific work shows that people who are more at risk for developing serious illnesses are those who display these patterns of behavior:

- They have unresolved emotional issues that consume their thoughts.

- They lack effective coping mechanisms to help them deal with emotional stress.

- They tend to view life from a negative perspective and advocate pessimism.

- They're often consumed with worry and are fearful that something bad is going to happen to them or to the people they love.

- They're unable to give and receive love, and they lack self-love.

- They're overly controlling and have a difficult time going with the flow.

- They laugh very little or engage infrequently in activities that develop their sense of humor.

- They take life too seriously and have unrealistic self-expectations.

- They suffer emotionally and see challenges as obstacles rather than opportunities to change.

- They have a tendency to deny themselves the things that can improve their quality of life.

- They don't tend to the needs of their body by feeding it properly or giving it sufficient rest.

- They lack mental flexibility and the ability to make course corrections when needed.

- They continue to make choices for other people's reasons and not their own.

- They have a difficult time expressing their emotional needs or asking for what they require.

- They're unable to establish healthy boundaries around what behavior is acceptable to them.

- They see their lives as not having meaning and experience bouts of hopelessness.

- They resist change and are unwilling to let go of the past.

- They don't believe that stress affects the body or that it contributes to the formation of illness.

I'm sure all of us have fit at least a few of these descriptions at some point over the course of our lives. I know that I have and still do. However, my reason for listing these behavioral patterns isn't to imply that if we exhibit them we're going to develop a serious disorder. It's only to point out that if we display them for a prolonged period of time, we increase the chances of developing an illness, while at the same time continuing to engage in habits and lifestyles that aren't conducive to creating the life and the health we desire. It's to underscore how, when we engage in unhealthy behavior, we lose our enthusiasm for life and affect our soul's ability to heal us.

What This Book Is About

This book is about sharing what I've learned about illness and healing as a medical intuitive over the course of 25 years of doing private sessions, working with both allopathic physicians and holistic practitioners; and 15 years of active research, studying, interviewing, and observing the workings of the relationship between the soul, energy body, mind, and physical self. It's my attempt to integrate scientific knowledge with esoteric wisdom so that both a rational and philosophical approach to healing can be considered, and I can offer a well-rounded perspective of what causes illness.

Healing Happens with Your Help is about uncovering the hidden contributors behind it so that you can address all of the factors responsible for its formation. I seek to offer an in-depth understanding of why you become ill, as well as providing tools that can be used to facilitate and accelerate the healing process. Within the contents of the book are mapping charts that I've developed over the years—charts that reveal where suppressed emotions and fears are stored energetically in the body's organs, glands, muscles, and in the plexus of the spine. I want you to be able to see where negative emotions such as anger, resentment, hostility, grief, disappointment, shame, and guilt are stored.

This book is about arming you with the knowledge that I hope will make it easier for you to let go of the emotional hurts that are stored in your body and transform them into tools that will empower and offer encouragement. It will present a comprehensive picture of all of the causes of illness.

I also want to share how important it is to remain open and receptive to all available modalities. The ideal healing model is the one that integrates the best that allopathic medicine has to offer with the best of holistic medicine. I think it's important to give the soul, mind, and body whatever each needs in order to restore balance among them. I've sat across from many people who are anti-medicine and who have chosen not to integrate what it offers into their healing modality and who have lost their fight with illness. And I've been with many people who are against holistic medicine and later wished that they'd looked into what it offered because it does work.

Our best course of action is to explore and research what's available because allopathic medicine and its technological advances are making it possible to live longer and remain healthier. In the case of cancer, you can explore chemotherapy, radiation, and surgery as well as some of the latest holistic approaches such as high dosages of vitamin C administered in the form of drips, hyperbaric oxygenation, homeopathy, Chinese medicine, liver and colon cleanses, and chelation therapy. Don't let conditioning, prejudices, and other people's opinions limit how you choose to heal yourself.

This book is about awakening your inner healer and learning how to liberate yourself from the thoughts, emotions, attitudes, beliefs, and core themes that prevent you from having a joyful life or expressing your uniqueness. It's about taking responsibility for your own healing and remembering that other people can merely support the process. They can't heal you—only you can do that.

What This Book Isn't About

What this book *isn't* about is assigning blame, guilt, or shame to ourselves or to other people for being ill or for not being able to heal. While it's part of our conditioning to try to do things right in everyone's eyes, it's virtually impossible. Why? Because "right" lies in the eyes of the beholder, meaning that what we consider correct may be light years apart from someone else's beliefs. It's based on each person's perceptions of what's acceptable, and frankly, the idea of "being right" is a manipulative tool to keep us behaviorally controlled. Instead of striving toward that goal, perhaps we should aim to be authentic. When we approach life and our health from that perspective, we don't suppress our emotions, nor do we devalue ourselves. We allow our strengths and uniqueness to find voices, and we become empowered and engaged with our inner healers. We move from blaming to commending ourselves for hanging in there and never giving up when the going gets rough. We accept ourselves, which is the first step in the healing process.

This book isn't intended to be a formal or technical treatise, but rather a compilation of my observations of the wisdom offered by the ancient physicians, metaphysicians, and alchemists regarding their perception of what's needed in order to heal. They saw illness as merely a disconnection between the soul, the mind, and the body. I'll share how their treatment protocols began by restoring the mental state, thus allowing the body to experience relief.

The pages that follow also aren't about curing, for all that does is to restore the body back to where it was before it became ill. In the end, that does little to address the underlying cause of illness, nor does it prevent recurrences.

How to Use This Book

There are numerous self-help books on how to heal and understand illness, which offer suggestions and techniques that guide the reader on how to change thoughts, emotions, attitudes, and beliefs that are preventing them from enjoying the health they desire. Even the pharmaceutical giants are jumping on the bandwagon by offering books, newsletters, and natural remedies to help understand and relieve symptoms and discomfort and treat minor health issues. Taking this into consideration, I've tried to make this book different by writing it more as a reference tool that you can use to understand the hidden contributors behind illnesses, to help you determine what steps you can take to facilitate the healing process.

A word about my style: I've chosen to use the word *illness* rather than *disease* as allopathic medicine does, because illness involves the soul as well as the mind and the body. Disease refers only to the physical. I use the word *brain* in some situations and *mind* in others because the brain is the organ responsible for sending the electrochemical messages between the soul, the mind, and the body. The mind, on the other hand, encompasses all thoughts, emotions, attitudes, beliefs, perceptions, and core themes—all of the elements affecting behavior that have an impact on the health and well-being of the body. The brain is structure and the mind is functionality.

I've also avoided medical jargon because I don't believe it's necessary. In fact, I think most diagnoses offered by allopathic medicine will make us even sicker because we're not sure what they mean or what their impact is. Take, for example the term *pseudofolliculitis barbe*. Sounds bad, doesn't it? In actuality, it's ingrown beard hairs. Point made.

The book is organized into three parts. The first two offer a comprehensive yet theoretical perspective of illness and healing. They review many of the hidden psychological contributors responsible for the formation of illness and seek to integrate scientific knowledge with esoteric wisdom used by many of the ancient metaphysicians and physicians of Egypt, Greece, and China.

The last part may feel like a completely different book. It's where you'll take what you've learned in the first two parts and apply it to the workings of the physical body. The information offered in this section is practical and can immediately be put to use in your quest for good health.

Here's a more detailed overview of each part, for your reference:

Part I, "Understanding the Nature of Healing," offers a new and different perspective—a psychospiritual viewpoint. It explores the difference between curing and healing and the difference between the soul and the spirit. This section includes the Seven Universal Tenets of Healing and direction as to how to use them and live by them.

Part II, "Discovering What's Really Behind Illness," delves into all of the underlying contributors of illness—thoughts, emotions, attitudes, beliefs, perceptions, and core themes—and breaks each down into palatable, bite-size pieces so you can begin to understand how they impact the health and well-being of the body. It explores the perception of illness from four divergent perspectives and reveals how each one influences not only which healing modalities are most effective in the healing process, but also the level of participation required in the process.

Part III, "Working with the Body for Optimal Health," connects the psychological contributors of illness to the structure and functioning of the body parts and systems. It reveals where in the body we store these contributors and how the body uses them to alert us when they're impeding its ability to function properly. This part of the book includes my Ritberger Body Mapping Charts™ that reveal where emotions, attitudes, beliefs, and fears are stored energetically in the organs, glands, muscles, and spine; there are visual representations as well as written descriptions. Also included in this part is a reference source with information on some of the most common illnesses and their hidden meanings: a general description; the hidden psychological implications associated with it; the emotions connected to it; whether the disconnection involves the soul, mind, or the body or if it's a combination; and what you can change to help restore good health.

The last chapter, "Steps for Healing Yourself," goes beyond the exploration and reference material of the preceding sections to offer the three steps you can take to change your health and your life. Its contents are rich with suggestions that can feed the needs of the soul, the mind, and the body.

Overall, the book is about creating a new psychospiritual model of healing. It's about changing the perception of illness from separateness to wholeness, from external to internal, acknowledging that the soul is inseparable from the body and the mind and that when all are working in a cooperative and unified manner then we sustain good health.

Seeing Illness Through a Different Set of Eyes

In the evolution of all things, it takes some sort of catalyst to start the momentum that triggers change. In this case, there has been a profound transformation in how people see their illnesses and the role they want to take in the healing process. Instead of turning over the responsibility of treatment and healing to physicians as has been done for years, there's an evolving group that has decided to take it upon themselves to participate in their own healing and who are recognizing there are other factors that need to be addressed if true healing is to occur. People are now realizing that scientific-based medicine is unable to give them the answers they need in order to understand what's causing their conditions, so they're turning to medical intuitives, holistic practitioners, and integrative physicians who offer a more complete picture and different forms of treatments.

This shift in perception has created an explosive growth

in the holistic and complementary fields of medicines because these modalities treat the soul, mind, and body and view the three as inseparable. They seek to uncover the underlying psychological factors that contribute to the formation of illness and work on changing both the mental state and the physical state. Even in a recent survey conducted by a national holistic association, it was found that one-third of those questioned had sought the assistance of a nontraditional source to help them understand their illnesses and to identify ways in which they could better participate in their own healing.

As we learn more, it quickly becomes obvious that it's imperative to change how illness is viewed. Perhaps what this shift in thinking is trying to tell us is that it's time to re-create the model of healing the ancient physicians, metaphysicians, and alchemists used to diagnose and treat. Perhaps it's time we set aside the differences in perception and the biases around healing and get back to the approach that has been successful for thousands of years. Better yet, let's expand it and create a new model of healing that:

- Blends the best of what allopathic and holistic medicine offer and brings into the healing equation the psychospiritual perspective, which seeks to restore the homeostasis between the soul, the mind, and the body

- Specifically offers treatment options that are designed to work with the individual's perception of illness and that will encourage them to actively participate in their own healing process

- Is focused on healing versus curing

- Acknowledges and understands how the mental and emotional states affect the physical and vice versa

- Has its prime directive focused on the soul and elicits the natural curative powers that are inherently a part of a person's divine nature

- Accepts the interconnectedness and interrelationship between the soul, the energy body, the mind, and the physical self and whose intention is to uncover the thoughts, emotions, attitudes, beliefs, and core themes that are disrupting the well-being of all

- Will at last reconcile the differences in the perception of illness, and that can settle the commonplace notions about how psychological factors can affect the health of the physical body

Will this new model of healing be better? It depends on who you talk to and their perception of illness. If you ask those who follow the thinking of allopathic medicine, don't be surprised if you get a negative reaction. On the other hand, if you put the question to those who are involved in holistic and integrative medicine, you'll get positive feedback. But the real beneficiary from this change is *you*. If you choose to transform your perceptions, change your thoughts, and do what you can to eliminate the hidden contributors behind illness, then not only will you enjoy good health, you'll be able to delight in a good life.

I hope this book will help you take that all-important first step on your personal healing journey.

❧ ✣ ❧

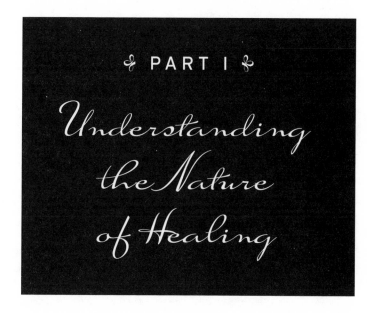

❦ PART I ❦

Understanding the Nature of Healing

*"Healing of the physical without the change
in the mental and spiritual aspects brings
little real help to the individual in the end."*
— Edgar Cayce

*"The doctor of the future will give no medicine, but
will instruct his patient in the care of the human frame,
in diet and in the cause and prevention of disease."*
— Thomas Edison

"That greatest miracle of all is the human being."
— Marya Mannes, from *More in Anger*

CHAPTER 1

Healing and Curing Aren't the Same

How many times have you heard someone announce, "I've been cured of cancer," or been told, "I just read about a new cure for that disease"? While it's certainly exciting that medicine, medical research, and technology can effectively rid the body of many of the illnesses that only 20 or 30 years ago would have resulted in death, they still can't effectively teach us how to heal or actually mend what ails us. Why? Curing and healing *are not* the same—not in their approach, what they require of the patient, or their results. Unfortunately, even with all of the advances, medicine is still measuring itself on curing, meaning restoring the body back to the state it was in before it became ill. It's not looking at healing, getting the body back to better than it was before it became ill, because all the causes of the illness have been addressed.

However, that's about to change as more and more people are becoming better educated about wellness and health and are realizing that their conditions require more than just seeing a doctor. There's an exciting opportunity presenting itself that can and will change the way we deal with illness. We're on the threshold of creating a new model of healing that will not only change the diagnosis methods, but will transform treatment, too.

Yet if we were to look back into the history of medicine, we'd find that this approach isn't really new at all. Instead, it's timeless in the sense that it begins where it should—with the healing of the soul and giving it what it needs so that we can live healthy, joyful lives. Rather than trying only to relieve the physical body of its symptoms, discomforts, aches, and pains, it seeks to remove the underlying contributors behind illness. These factors are responsible for preventing the soul—the core essence of who we are—from finding its physical expression through our thoughts, words, and behaviors—they cause us to compromise who we are and create distorted self-perceptions. This model aims to remove the unhealthy thoughts, emotions, attitudes, beliefs, perceptions, and core themes that create an unhealthy mental and physical state. It restores the balance between the mind, body, spirit, and soul—it doesn't just cure the ailments of the physical self.

Throughout almost every civilization in history, there are records describing how metaphysicians, alchemists, hermetists, shamans, medicine men, and even great physicians of Greece approached healing from a psychospiritual perspective, meaning that they began at the soul level and worked from the inside out to the ailments and malfunctioning of the body. Writings by Hermes, Paracelsus, Plato, Fludd, Descartes, and even Hippocrates—considered the Father of Western Medicine—described how the healing of the body must begin by removing the contributors that are preventing a person's soul from doing its divine work. All agreed that illness was the disconnection from our spiritual nature, and all believed that when the unhealthy thoughts and unnatural behavior were addressed and eliminated, the physical body would return to its natural state of balance and the individual would once again experience good health.

Through their individual models of humanity's divine nature and of healing, they collectively showed that if restoration was to occur, then the mind, body, and soul must function in a cooperative unified manner, thus freeing the soul to do its true work. They also showed that there is a subtle, invisible energy body within us that surrounds and interpenetrates the physical, and that it is so sensitive to our thoughts that if they're unhealthy it will protect us by causing a disconnection to occur among the three aspects of the self. They referred to this break as illness, and believed that the problem would show up as a *pre-illness* in this nonvisible energy body, which could be seen by those possessing clairvoyant abilities.

Consistently, there are references throughout their works about how the nonvisible and physical bodies are duplications of each other, so what affects one has an impact on the other, and how curing and healing are not the same. Their consensus was that curing only worked on the physical body, while healing worked on all aspects—mental, emotional, physical, and spiritual.

Curing

The focus of curing is to address the needs of the physical body and to relieve it of any discomfort, aches and pains, symptoms, crises, and illness. It has little to do with treating the hidden contributors responsible for the formation of these effects. Instead, curing views good health as the absence of symptoms and the elimination of whatever is causing the body to not function properly, even if that means removing a part of the body. This approach means compensation and removal. For example, if a person is experiencing muscle cramps, the treatment is relaxants; if pain is present, then painkillers are prescribed. If the body is burning up with a fever, curing seeks to cool it down; and if cancer is present, curing removes it.

While this method certainly makes it easier for us to live physically, it doesn't address the origin of the problem, only the effects. As a result, the perpetrators are still there and are continuing to gain strength, thus weakening the body's ability to sustain good health.

Curing looks at the *how* and *what* of illness. It views the body as a biomechanical piece of machinery, where most parts are necessary but may not be connected or interdependent on the other parts for proper functioning. It sees organs, glands, and systems and wants to understand *how* they break down and *what* can be replaced or repaired to eliminate the problem. It doesn't take the mental state into consideration.

Yet curing does play an important role by giving a physical and mental reprieve from discomfort by using medications or surgery. This offers both the mind and the body time to try to restore some state of balance. Let me explain. When the body hurts, the role of the mind is to try to understand the problem. However, this isn't as easy as it sounds because of the presence of pain. Anytime something hurts, the mind forgets what it's supposed to do. Instead, it fixates on the anguish, which causes the brain to release more pain receptors. They escalate the urgency that the mind feels and distract it even more by flooding it chemically to the point that it's immobilized. This turns the process of trying to restore balance into a vicious cycle, with the body being caught in the middle. At this point, the mind and the body are both so receptive to anything that will help them remember what it feels like to be pain free that we'll find ourselves grabbing over-the-counter or prescription drugs or whatever else it takes, even if we wouldn't normally like using such methods.

Curing supports taking a passive role and encourages delegating the healing process to someone else. The relationship between the caregiver and patient is often one of authority and dependence, and in most cases, the patient is presumed to be incapable of making informed choices. As a result, those decisions are assigned to the caregiver, with the patient following orders. Although physicians are well trained and very skilled at their profession, such a scenario doesn't foster healing because it doesn't encourage active participation.

Since curing focuses on the body, it rarely takes our spiritual nature into consideration. It doesn't acknowledge the presence of the energy body or the role of the soul. Even though the caregiver may believe in both and understand their importance, the diagnostics and treatment forms of curing don't.

Healing

Healing, on the other hand, begins with the soul and seeks to identify, transform, and remove any obstacles preventing it, the mind, and the body from working together in a unified manner. The objective is to make us better than we were before we became ill and to reestablish "wholeness" so that we can experience good health. It involves creating a harmonious internal space so we can explore the hidden contributors behind illness at a deeper level. We get in touch with who we are and are allowed to see just how powerful we can be if we free ourselves from the limitations of our conditioning.

Healing views health as being physically, mentally, emotionally, and spiritually in balance. The organs, glands, and systems of the body don't suffer stress or emotional strain; and the mind is released from mental barriers and distorted self-perceptions. The soul is free of the obstacles preventing it from finding physical expression. Healing deals with the source of illness and requires us to dig into our psychological coffers so we can uncover unhealthy thoughts, emotions, attitudes, beliefs, and core themes responsible for the formation of illness. It's about reinventing our self-perception and restructuring our lifestyle so that it's conducive to good health. We remove the sources responsible for the disconnection between the soul, mind, and body.

Healing begins with awareness and ends with change. It asks us to release the emotional hurts buried deep inside and let go of the identities we've created around those hurts. We must give up our habits and comfort zones and renounce unhealthy behavior that compromises who we really are, even if that behavior makes us feel safe or helps us resemble everyone else. Those who place more value on logic are asked to shift their perceptions and learn to embrace their emotional nature, even if that means having occasional outbursts. On the other hand, naturally expressive individuals are required to learn to deal objectively with their emotions and to stop victimizing themselves with stories of how they've been hurt. This method asks overly controlling people to let go of their need to be constantly in charge and allow other people to help them. And it requests that passive folks become actively involved in their health rather than allowing others to control what happens to them.

Healing supports taking an active role in the care of the body and discourages delegating what happens to it. It requires commitment, determination, and asking others for help; it creates cooperative relationships and fosters trust. The caregiver and the patient work as a team, discussing, exploring, researching, and trying alternatives in addition to standard treatments. There's no authoritarian role, nor does the caregiver choose the correct route. Instead, that person sees patients as part of the decision-making process, ultimately responsible for the choices concerning their health.

The goal of healing isn't fixing, it's creating—creating a healthy self-perception, healthy thoughts, and healthy relationships. This approach embodies the qualities of the soul, such as loving, accepting, appreciating, compassion, patience, and tolerance. It honors our spiritual nature and acknowledges our efforts through good health. It liberates us from our past so that we're free to create anew. This is an ongoing process of self-discovery and spiritual evolution that involves laughing, crying, playing, being silly, and being spontaneous. It's a return to being the child who was eager to learn and to engage in the experiences of life for the sheer pleasure of finding out what's possible.

However, healing can also seem difficult and uncomfortable at times, as the past and all of its dysfunction bubbles to the surface. In fact, there may be points in the process when we find ourselves asking whether we can really do it or if it's worth the effort. However, if we persevere, we'll be amazed by how many wonderful memories we'll find in the mire and the muck. We'll be astounded by how much we've accomplished and truly how rich our lives have been. We'll find ourselves feeling good about who we are, and we'll have the opportunity to touch a part of ourselves that's more precious that anything we can ever acquire externally. We'll make contact with our souls.

If we can remember that healing is a way of life and not something we just strive to achieve when we're ill, then we'll be more inclined to live intelligently, simply, honorably, efficiently, and in alignment with our spiritual nature. Each day will then become a healing event.

The Psychospiritual Approach to Healing

In his writings, Edgar Cayce best described the principles of psychospiritual healing when he said, "Spirit is the life. Mind is the builder. Physical is the result." This approach sees healing as a co-creative process among the soul, the mind, and the body; and sees illness as a breakdown in the process. It understands such a problem as representing something deeper, happening internally, that's weakening the body's defenses so it becomes vulnerable to the external contributors of illness—such as viruses, bacterial infections, environmental contaminants, or something ingested. Psychospiritual healing views illness as the soul's way of alerting the mind that something we're thinking isn't in alignment with our spiritual nature, and immediate change is required before it affects the body.

This approach to healing works on three premises:

1. An unhealthy mental state contributes to an unhealthy physical state.

2. Healing only occurs when unresolved issues at a psychological level are identified and removed.

3. Only we can heal ourselves. No one else can.

This model delves deeper into the connection between illness and thoughts, emotions and beliefs, perceptions and core themes; and takes into consideration how all of these factors affect the relationship between the soul, the mind, and the body. Its objective is to show us how to identify the unhealthy contributors buried deep within our psychological coffers, how to remove these problems and release their emotional charges, and how to tap into our spiritual nature so the healing qualities of the soul and spirit can be released. This approach facilitates healing on a higher level.

CHAPTER 2

Healing on a Higher Level

The ultimate objective of healing is to assist the soul in its evolutionary process, meaning removing any obstacles preventing our spiritual nature from being experienced and expressed fully and joyfully in our thoughts, words, and actions. Yet in order for this objective to be accomplished, there are five major shifts in perceptions we must make.

1. We must shift the perception we have of ourselves and see ourselves as more than just physical bodies. We need to remember that we exist on two dimensions—that of matter, the physical body and the mind, and that of energy, the spirit and the soul. Our spiritual nature comprises all.

2. Rather than just seeing illness causing problems in the physical body, we need to understand that it has an impact on the mind, in the energy body, and in the soul as well. We

need to view it as a breakdown in the interaction and communication between all of these aspects of who we are.

3. Instead of seeing thoughts as being self-contained within the confines of our brain, we should know that they're the energetic attractors of our experiences, and the ultimate determinants of the health and well-being of the physical body.

4. We need to see experiences as related and connected, not random and disconnected. We must realize that all experiences—both good and bad—play an integral role in the evolutionary process.

5. We must come to understand that the soul and spirit aren't the same, even though the words are often used interchangeably. We need to recognize that although it's intangible, the soul is still the impetus behind the evolutionary process and serves as the catalyst for change. In contrast, the spirit functions as the energetic lifeline between the soul, the mind, and the body.

The Soul

The soul is our core essence, the source of our aliveness. It serves as our inner navigator as we move through life, guiding us forward on our evolutionary journey. It provides the energetic vitality that animates the physical body and helps sustain us in our darkest times by offering us comfort, hope, and inspiration. This is our inner healer that oversees the functioning of the body when we're ill.

The soul speaks to us through the voice of intuition, offering an endless flow of possibilities and alerting us if our thoughts are unhealthy or we've put ourselves in harm's way. It contains the archival history of all that we have experienced on the physical earth plane—both in this current lifetime and in past incarnations.

The soul can't be seen, but it's experienced through the living matter of our body and in our thoughts. It uses both as a means of physical expression, thus allowing our spiritual nature to be seen and experienced in the outer world. The soul has been described in many religious teachings as the Heart of God, the Celestial Chariot connecting us with the Source and the Universe, and the vehicle for personal evolution and spiritual development. It focuses on quality of life and the relationships we develop. As we move forward through the cycles of existence, the soul energetically records what we've learned from our experiences in our cells and in our energy body. These lessons are of the greatest value; they're the true gifts of life.

The soul harnesses the thoughts of the mind to let us know when we're in alignment with our spiritual nature and when we're not. It accomplishes this through emotions: When we're happy, joyful, and content, we're in alignment. When we're angry, depressed, and discontented, we aren't. These messages are easy to read—all we have to do is tune in to our emotions.

Aches, pains, discomfort, tension, stress, emotional crises, symptoms, and illness are the soul's ways of bringing attention to unhealthy thoughts. They're intended to heighten our awareness that there's some degree of resistance, reluctance, or unwillingness to change old patterns, let go of the past, and move beyond our comfort zones and habits. When we experience any of these indicators, it's never the soul's intention to cause bodily harm. It understands that in our humanness, we're susceptible to creating thought-forms that cause limitations in thinking. We're prone to bury emotional hurts that feed our fear of change and create self doubt. It knows that in order to move forward in our personal growth and spiritual development, we sometimes need more than a gentle nudge, so it uses symptoms and discomfort as a way of showing us what needs to change.

In the evolutionary process, it's the soul that originates our experiences and determines our divine work, giving us the opportunity to learn, grow, and transcend unhealthy ways of thinking. This lets us change limiting patterns of behavior that are preventing us from having the health and life we desire. When the energy of the soul separates from the body in death, all that's left is a physical shell that begins to deteriorate and decompose immediately. The soul then returns to its energetic nature and waits for the next opportunity to revitalize itself again in a physical body.

The Spirit

The spirit is the energetic lifeline that connects the soul, the mind, and the physical body. It's the communication interface among the three and makes it possible for the soul to express its intentions through human experience. The spirit is the aura, and it forms the energy body that surrounds and interpenetrates the physical body. It's vibrational in nature and uses its wavelike frequencies and energy patterns to reveal the sojourns of the soul and to *magnetically* attract experiences that promote personal growth and advance the soul in its evolutionary process.

It can't be seen, but is experienced through the living matter of the physical body. Even though it's an interface with the mind, it doesn't contribute to the thoughts we create the way the soul does. Rather, it's merely the vehicle that broadcasts those thoughts to the external world and then receives them back in the form of energy-carrying information that falls below the threshold of our physical senses.

The spirit occupies the same space as the physical body and creates the electromagnetic framework for the soul. This structure, even though invisible, mirrors the physical body and connects the soul and the body inseparably. Consequently, what affects one affects the other. As unhealthy thoughts break down the physical self's defenses and leave it susceptible to illness, they also destroy the spirit's energy and leave it susceptible to blockages that diminish its capacity to serve as the interface for the soul, mind, and body.

The spirit is the energetic interpreter of the soul's intentions, and is responsible for distributing them throughout the body. The vibration of the spirit, as with the soul, is more intimately connected to the part of the brain that uses symbolism and metaphors and relies on emotions for feedback. It's the neutral liaison between the soul and the mind, and its primary responsibility is to see that what we create mentally is transmitted externally. This lets us attract our thoughts back in the form of experiences. The spirit and the soul make up the energy body, which is an internal reflection of what's happening on the outside.

The spirit doesn't just see how illness is affecting the physical body. It puts things in a broader context, meaning how the problem is affecting the soul's ability to accomplish its evolutionary objectives. It uses its vibrational nature to influence the body to remove any obstacles preventing the soul from its physical expression. While the spirit can't influence the quality of the thoughts we create, it can mirror how they're affecting us mentally, emotionally, and physically. This brings attention to a disconnection among the soul, mind, and body. The rupture can manifest in fatigue, discomfort, mental confusion, emotional outbursts, and depression.

Upon death, the spirit provides the vehicle for the soul to transition from the body back into light and energy.

The Energy Body . . .
a Microcosm of the Physical Body

In its complexity of organs, glands, and systems, our physical body has a multidimensional feedback system that helps monitor and regulate how it's functioning. The energy body provides an instant readout of what's happening physically as well as mentally; its flow reflects how each is affecting the other. It's responsible for sustaining the life force that moves throughout the physical self and for directing the body in how to absorb and distribute the effects of our thoughts, emotions, attitudes, and beliefs into the cells, muscles, organs, glands, and all of the major systems.

The energy body not only oversees all energetic, electrochemical, and metabolic activities of the physical body, it supervises how all of these factors are affecting the interaction of the soul, mind, and body. In effect, it's a duplicate of all three, and through its information provides a comprehensive picture of what's happening energetically in all of them. The data reveals:

- If the systems, organs, and glands are functioning properly, and if not, which ones are malfunctioning and how they're affecting the body overall

- How stress and external factors are affecting the physical self

- If energy is flowing freely throughout the body, and if not, where specifically it's blocked, congested, or depleted

- If there are any psychological contributors affecting the interaction and communication process of the soul, mind, and body and whether a disconnection is being created

- Where the breakdown is occurring and how it's affecting the physical body—meaning, whether it's affecting only individual organs and glands or the major systems and their components

- What the root cause of the disconnection is—unhealthy thoughts, attitudes, beliefs, or behavioral patterns

- What must be done in order to restore balance to the physical body so that it can heal itself and reestablish communication with the soul and mind

The energy body provides much information on the health of the physical self and how the soul's intentions are being integrated into its physiology. The psychospiritual approach to healing places a tremendous value on this information, using it to uncover the hidden contributors behind illness and discover where they're being energetically stored.

A Highly Developed Communication Network

The energy body is a highly developed communication network that's in constant contact with all of the systems of the physical body. It's the common interface through which we interact with *everything,* both externally and internally. It serves as an antenna, transmitting and receiving energy-carrying information through its vibrational frequencies.

When the energy body is in external transmission mode, it's broadcasting our thoughts and the intentions of the soul into the outer world. The messages it's sending seek to attract experiences that match what we're thinking and that will promote personal growth and move us forward in the evolutionary process. In the external receiving mode, the components of the energy body, the soul, the heart, the chakras, the vascular autonomic system, and the central nervous system are all taking in the energy-carrying outside information. They're translating it, distributing it, and energetically absorbing it into the organs, glands, muscles, and bones as thought memories that determine how these parts of the body provide feedback and will respond in the future.

On the other hand, when the energy body is in the internal transmission mode, it's requesting the current status of the physical body, the soul, and our mental state. In the internal receiving mode, the energy body takes its collected information and serves as a feedback system. If it gets the message that one or more aspects of who we are have ceased functioning in a healthy way, it will distribute that data. It will also request that the mind check it out and identify the problem and that the body fix the problem.

For the most part, we're unaware mentally and physically of the workings of the energy body and only notice its activities when there's a problem. At that point, we experience it physically—through fatigue, muscle tension, and stress—and mentally in the form of emotional distress and confusion.

When Thoughts Change—Energy Changes

There are many situations within our daily lives that have an effect on our body's ability to heal itself. However, the one that has the greatest impact is thought. As Edgar Cayce said, "The mind is the builder," and when its contents are toxic then the physical and energy bodies are poisoned. And contrary to what we may think, it only takes one strong negative thought to begin the process.

The adage "Energy flows where intention goes" explains the phenomena that thoughts are the source of where we place our energies, and our energies are where we place our thoughts. Let me explain. Thoughts are energy, and they develop patterns that are carried throughout the energy body for external transmission. They also move through the energy body internally seeking feedback on how a new thought is affecting the physical body and its functioning.

In its internal search for information, the energy body scans the organs, glands, and major systems of the physical body to see if any of them hold a similar memory. If they do, then they provide the feedback on whether this new thought is healthy, meaning it's not causing any disconnection between the soul and body, or if it's unhealthy and creating a disturbance in the energy body and a disconnection between the soul and the physical. Once that feedback is received, it's sent electrochemically to the mind for evaluation. Unhealthy information gives the mind a message charged with stress and physical discomfort, and a healthy response sends a general sense of overall well-being.

The mind has the option of acting on what it has received, either changing the thought or producing similar ones. It may choose the latter option if the idea appears to supports old attitudes, beliefs, and core themes. However, just because thoughts are familiar doesn't mean they're necessarily healthy, which is the case with chronic illnesses. Most of them represent some sort of decay—either the disintegration of unhealthy thoughts or the breakdown of the body as the result of such ideas.

Conditions such as arthritis; digestive problems; heart disease; autoimmune disorders, including lupus, chronic fatigue, and fibromyalgia; and even cancer are the body's way of warning the mind that it's time to let go of the thought patterns that are creating an unhealthy mental state. These illnesses reveal how years of such thoughts tear the body down to the point that it's succumbing to the ravages of prolonged stress. They also show us how these patterns are impacting the energy body's ability to get an accurate reading on the physical self, and to provide the feedback needed to keep the soul, mind, and body healthy and communicating effectively with each other.

The Truth about Healing

There's an old philosophical truth about healing: *It's not just a science, it's a way of living.* It should happen every moment, not just when we become fearful that some ache or symptom might be an indicator of something more serious. Enjoying a healthful life requires that we align our outward experiences with the intentions of our soul. It requires that our thoughts reflect our needs, and not the demands and desires of other people or our conditioning. By merely managing what we think, we'll create a life that supports good health. If we're experiencing illness, healing requires that we look inside ourselves for the hidden motives behind creating unhealthy thoughts. If we're healthy, then we should still analyze what we're thinking as a preventive measure. If the thoughts are out of alignment, we must change them, even if it's uncomfortable.

Healing asks us to evaluate our relationships to see if they foster problematic thoughts. Sometimes this means letting go of outdated or codependent connections and creating new ones. It requires that we develop our intuition because it's the voice of our soul and will make it easier for us to read the messages of the energy body and the physical body. We need to expand our perception of healing and see it more as freeing ourselves from all of the contributors behind illness, even those that are buried deep within the recesses of our mind and in our body.

Most important, a healing life asks us to live filled with the gentleness and grace of the spirit and the compassion and love of the soul—for these are the greatest healers of all, and serve as the fundamental tenets behind the divine art of healing.

CHAPTER 3

The Divine Art of Healing

If we were to look at our body as being the tip of the iceberg, we'd understand that what we see is just a very small part of what determines whether we're in good health. There's much below the surface that plays such an integral part in the wholeness of our entire structure; and unless we become ill, we might not even be aware of its existence. The metaphor of the iceberg allows us to understand what it takes to enjoy a healthy life and to see that what affects the body is more than what meets the eye. It illustrates that good health is more than addressing just the needs of the physical body, but concerns the needs of the soul and the mind as well. It reveals why healing is a way of living and being.

Using the image of the iceberg, the layer directly below the surface is behavior, which represents how we act, what we do, what we eat, how we interact with other people, how we manage the stressors in our life, how we take care of ourselves, and how we safeguard ourselves against illness. If our patterns support a balanced lifestyle and meet the needs of the soul, mind, and body, then we experience good health. However, if our behavior is self-sabotaging, keeps us locked into detrimental patterns of thinking, and supports bad habits, then we increase our susceptibility to illness. We're also less inclined to be in touch with our body or to act as quickly as needed in changing any behavior that undermines its health.

Right below the behavior layer is where we'll find beliefs, which are repetitive thoughts that have become fixed in our minds, and core themes, which are beliefs that have become fixed in our behavior. Beliefs are responsible for the formation of habits and comfort zones and are difficult to change because the mind thinks they're true. Consequently, it will support them even at the expense of undermining both our mental and physical state.

Core themes cause us to perpetuate the beliefs formed by conditioning, social customs, interactions with other people, financial circumstances, and family expectations. Both beliefs and core themes are responsible for unnatural behavior and are the source of our mental and physical discomfort and emotional suffering. They distort our perception of reality.

The next layer of the iceberg represents our emotional state, and comprises both emotions and attitudes. It's in this layer that we discover our general outlook on life and find the wounded inner child. This section reveals how conditioning has affected the way we feel about ourselves and how our interactions with other people have affected our self-worth and self-esteem. This is the location of our fears and our strong attachments to them. They affect the layers above, resulting in unhealthy beliefs and core themes and destructive behavior.

The layer below emotions represents our mental state. If the predominant thought patterns we create are in alignment with the intentions of the soul and the needs of the body, then the iceberg will move around freely. It will withstand rough times and the tip will remain upright. On the other hand, if the thought patterns we create are unhealthy—meaning they compromise who we are, create false and distorted self-perceptions, and are unsupportive of healthy behavior—then the foundation of the iceberg will be compromised and underdeveloped. Full of cracks, it will have a difficult time remaining stable.

The largest part of the iceberg and the part that's rarely seen is the spiritual layer, consisting of the energy body and the soul. This section serves as the foundation upon which healthy physical, mental, and emotional states are created. It holds within it the healing powers that can transform, transmute, and transcend illness. This is the layer of our spiritual nature and reflects the self that sees an evolutionary journey toward wholeness. The energy body and soul represent our way of being and our overall perception of life. This spiritual layer provides the guidance needed to restore good health mentally and physically. It answers the questions "Who am I?" and "What is my purpose for being?" It's the part of the iceberg that remains constantly stable and keeps the entire thing afloat even when the other layers chip away at its foundation. The spiritual layer is where the healing emotions of love and hope originate, along with the attitudes of forgiveness, optimism, and gratitude. These are all so powerful that they create instantaneous changes in the energy body and restore balance to all other parts.

However, the healing powers this layer offers are only accessible if the one above it—the layer of thoughts—embraces its existence and trusts that we can heal ourselves. To ensure this happens, the soul offers a method that changes any dysfunction on all layers simultaneously. All it takes is our willingness to alter our thoughts.

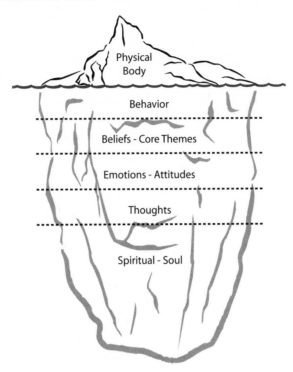

Physical
Body

Behavior

Beliefs - Core Themes

Emotions - Attitudes

Thoughts

Spiritual - Soul

The Model of Healing

The steps in this healing model—evaluation, education, orchestration, and liberation—are simple, transformative, easy to understand, simple to follow, and immediately applicable in any situation. Yet even in their simplicity, the impact they have on the soul, mind, and body is profound.

Evaluation

Evaluation is a self-diagnostic process that makes it possible for us to tune in to where we are mentally, emotionally, and physically at any given moment. It forces us to pay attention to how we're conducting our lives and to see if we're supporting good health or contributing to the wear and tear of stress on the physical body.

The evaluation of the mental state directs our attention inward and creates an environment where we can see ourselves beyond our mental limitations and conditioning. Its reflective nature allows us to eavesdrop on our self-talk to see if our inner conversations are critical, judgmental, or self-deprecating. If they're toxic, then our body will be, too. If they're self-destructive, then they'll disturb the natural balance of the soul, mind, and body and will cause a disconnection. Mental evaluation allows us to observe the quality of our thoughts and monitor how they're affecting our thoughts.

The evaluation of the emotional state allows us to uncover the hurts buried deep inside and see what fears we've attached to them. Once these are uncovered, we can look at our options. Do we continue to allow them to affect our life and keep us held hostage to our old emotional wounds? Or do we remove the charges attached to them—thus freeing ourselves from their hold—and begin to live in alignment with the needs of the soul, mind, and body?

The evaluation of the physical state makes it possible for us to take a realistic "pulse check" of how the body's feeling and functioning. Are there aches and pains, chronic health issues, or any change in our stamina? Are we getting enough rest? Is our diet conducive to good health and healing? Are we giving our body the exercise it needs? Are we managing our stress—or is it managing us?

Education

Illness is a great teacher because it forces us to learn more about why we think and act the way we do. It supports learning more about our personality, beliefs, core themes, fears, conditioning, biological history, strengths, weaknesses, and self-perceptions (both positive and negative). It encourages change, the exploration of possibilities, and finding ways to turn toxic situations into healthy ones.

Illness reveals how limited our view of reality really is and teaches us how important it is to uncover the unhealthy beliefs we have around well-being. In its presence we learn the importance of expressing our emotions and not keeping them buried deep inside just because we're afraid that other people won't like or accept us. Being ill offers us the opportunity to find effective ways to say how we feel and teaches us the importance of establishing healthy emotional boundaries.

When illness strikes, it clearly and succinctly tells us what's happening deep below the surface of our skin, encouraging us to learn more about how our body works and to observe what happens to it when we don't take care of it. Such an experience teaches us what foods we should eat to maintain vitality. We learn, for example, that when diets are high in sugar and simple carbohydrates, we seem to get sudden bursts of energy, yet they're immediately followed by extreme fatigue and a mental letdown. We learn about the effects of stress and how important it is to develop coping strategies so that we can minimize its effects.

Illness teaches us the importance of mental management and how the quality of our thoughts determines the quality of our health. It teaches us how important it is to try new things and to explore all of our options.

Orchestration

This step is where the rubber meets the road. At this point, it's full speed ahead in the fast lane of healing—change is inevitable. This is also the process that offers us the greatest opportunity to experience just how powerful we are.

After taking the time to evaluate and educate ourselves on what we must do to move forward in the healing process, the soul, mind, and body aren't supportive of a "wait and see" attitude. They're unlikely to allow us to perpetuate limiting thinking, unhealthy beliefs, bad habits, and self-destructive patterns of behavior. We can try, but the mental and emotional discomfort we'll experience is sometimes more uncomfortable than the aches and pains associated with the illness.

The orchestration process gives us the chance to try some of the options we discovered in the education step and to engage in activities supportive of good health. We have the opportunity to expand our awareness and enjoy the shift in our self-perceptions. In this part of the healing process, we'll find ourselves gaining a deeper appreciation for life and our relationships. How we act and think will change, and we'll evolve into the self-actualized people that Abraham Maslow spoke of in his influential book, *Toward a Psychology of Being.* He described self-actualized people as not being without the absence of problems, but being those who have learned to transmute those problems from the unreal into the real. These individuals have effectively orchestrated the necessary changes that caused their perception of illness to be transformed. They're liberated from the shackles of their past.

Liberation

This step in the healing process is the reward for our commitment and determination to continue through the steps, even though it might have been uncomfortable at times. This culminates in our ability to rise above and move beyond our current mental state. Liberation from our past allows us the opportunity to live life joyfully and without the pain and suffering caused by our emotional hurts. Free from distorted self-perceptions, we're able to discover who we really are and learn what we're capable of achieving.

Liberation expands how we think and how we relate to and interact with the outer world. We experience behavioral changes because how we act is no longer dictated by old beliefs and core themes. However, being liberated doesn't mean we forsake our past; we just channel its information in a different direction. Instead of allowing it to drive our life, we use its lessons as a means of discerning whether the behavior we're displaying is what we want it to be rather than what others think it should be.

Liberation serves as an incentive for us to let go of the old and create the new—fresh ways of thinking, being, and living and new methods to fulfill the needs of the soul, mind, and body. This takes what we've learned and melds it with the wisdom of our soul, which holds within its energy the Seven Universal Tenets of Healing.

The Seven Universal Tenets of Healing

1. You have the power to heal yourself. The physical body is designed for self-healing and comes equipped with a defense system that will ward off the external and internal contributors of illness. It's designed for self-regeneration by creating new cells daily. We can only stop this from happening when we believe it can't, and we don't give it what it needs: rest, proper nutrition, and exercise.

2. Only you can heal yourself. No one else can. Creating a healing team is of great value when dealing with an illness because the members can offer knowledge, suggestions, different perspectives, and most important, support. However, they can't heal you—only you can do that. It's a personal journey of self-discovery and spiritual evolution. No one else can experience your emotions, understand the workings of your mind, or create your thoughts. Others can help you recognize unhealthy patterns, but only you can change them.

3. Heal the soul first; then the healing of the mind and body will take place. The soul, mind, and body all have different needs; and if they get what they require, all remain healthy. However, if any of them is neglected, then there's a disconnection and all become unwell. Healing restores the connection among the soul, mind, and body. While the perspective of medicine is to deal with the body first, the divine art of healing reminds us to begin with the soul because it's the source of our being and animates the body and the mind. If we start here, then the others will follow automatically. What are the needs of the soul? They are to live a joyful and purposeful life, to grow personally, and to express its intentions through our thoughts, words, and actions.

4. Only love heals. The energy of love carries an incredible healing power. When you offer affection to any part of your body that's hurting or not functioning properly, it engages the restorative powers of the soul and the mind. There's a mental shift in attention from identifying a problem to finding solutions, and the soul embraces that part of the body and floods it with unconditional love. This emotion lives in the present moment, which is where healing occurs—it doesn't happen in the past or future.

5. Forgiveness creates the space for love in the heart. When our hearts are full of fear, anger, sadness, or despair, there's no room for caring, without which it's difficult to remain healthy. While love is associated with the soul, forgiveness is linked to the mind and represents the release of the emotional charges attached to hurtful thoughts—those that support victim behavior and cause us to live tentatively rather than fully. Forgiveness removes blocks in the energy body so that its information can flow freely and provide the feedback that the soul, mind, and body need in order to remain healthy. It vibrationally removes unhealthy beliefs and fears held in the spine, and toxic emotional charges in the organs, glands, and muscles. It begins the healing process and fortifies our immunity so we're less susceptible to the formation of illness.

6. Change is the only action plan. The evolutionary journey is one of change; there are no other options in life. This is what happens from one thought to another. Change reshapes our thinking and moves us from the past into the present and from the present into the future. The first step in transformation is forgiveness, and the next is love. When we forgive ourselves and those who have hurt us, we enlarge our mental space so that there's room for new thoughts, and we expand our hearts so we have a greater capacity for love. When we become ill, our soul, mind, and body are all asking for change. They're alerting us that something isn't working and that there's a disconnection among the three that's affecting their well-being. In the psychospiritual healing model offered by the soul, we're reminded that if our thoughts are ill, so is our body. The only way to heal both is to shift our thinking. Henri Bergson summed up the healing power of change when he said, "To exist is to change; to change is to mature, to mature is to go on creating oneself endlessly."

7. Focus on what you want rather than what you don't want. Healing works with the Law of Attraction: *What you think, you become. What you become, you think.* The best way to see whether your thoughts are healthy is to look at your lifestyle, relationships, and health. If what you see isn't what you want, then change it. There's a common ailment that plagues all of us at sometime in our life: We seem to attract what we don't want rather than what we do. This is because we're so focused on the thoughts we don't want that we're continually repeating them, while at the same time reinforcing them with strong negative emotions. It's kind of like trying not to think about a hippopotamus— the more we tell ourselves not to think about it, the more we do. Then as our thoughts increase, we get more and more upset with ourselves for not putting it out of our minds. Actually, the scenario is rather ridiculous—it's like a dog obsessed with chasing its tail. The only way to stop the process is to change it.

Illness Doesn't Just Happen Overnight

If we could change our perception of illness and understand that it develops over time, we might be more loving and forgiving toward ourselves and more patient with the healing process. We might even develop a different perception of what it takes to heal ourselves, and rather than looking to others to heal us, we'll take a more active role in the process by changing the things in our lives that aren't healthy.

Take cancer for example. This illness doesn't happen suddenly. Physically, it takes time to develop and manifest itself to the point that it can be found through diagnostic tests. It takes months—and in some cases, even years—for cells to mutate to the point they evolve into a tumor or mass. Mentally, it takes years of conditioning, functioning in an environment where unhealthy thoughts drive behavior, supporting detrimental habits, and remaining in a mental state that focuses on the negatives and life's problems. Emotionally, it takes years of suppressing emotions, maintaining the inability to express our emotional needs, compromising who we are, and allowing our hurts to affect the quality of our lives.

Illness—whether flu, a common cold, or something more serious such as cancer—is the result of an unhealthy mental state that has weakened the immune system over the course of time to the point that it loses its effectiveness in protecting the body either from external invaders (such as viruses or bacteria) or from internal threats (such as unhealthy thoughts and negative emotions and attitudes). It isn't something that just happens. It takes time.

If we learn to listen to the subtle messages the body sends us before they become urgent calls to action, we'll be able to significantly decrease our susceptibility to illness. We'll recognize that the body is constantly providing feedback on its current mental and physical status and that it can even tell us what we need to change in order to restore good health. However, it requires that we understand the nature of illness and discover what's really behind it.

PART II

Discovering What's Really Behind Illness

"The truth about our childhood is stored in our body, and although we can repress it, we can never alter it. Our intellect can be deceived, our feelings manipulated, our perceptions confused, and our body tricked with medications. But someday the body will present its bill, for it is as incorruptible as a child who, still whole in spirit, will accept no compromises or excuses, and will not stop tormenting us until we stop evading the truth."
— from *The Drama of the Gifted Child* by Alice Miller

"Emotion is the moment when steel meets flint and a spark is struck forth, for emotion is the chief source of consciousness. There is no change from darkness to light or from inertia to movement without emotion."
— from *The Archetypes and the Collective Unconscious* by Carl Jung

"People everywhere enjoy believing in that they know is not true. It spares them the ordeal of thinking for themselves and taking responsibility for what they know."
— from *Once Around the Sun* by Brooks Atkinson

CHAPTER 4

Everyone Has a Story

Can you remember back to when you were three years old . . . or 6 or 10 or 13? I sure can, but frankly I'd rather not. I was a precocious child who never seemed to grow beyond asking zillions of "why" questions. And as I recall those days, I can understand the reasons why my parents, teachers, and other people got so frustrated, upset, and angry with me. From my perspective, I was just trying to understand and learn . . . and show them how smart I was, because that was why I was praised.

I can remember my dad saying to his friends: "Carol is the bright one of my children and will be the first in our family to graduate from high school." He was so proud of me, and his saying that would make me feel really important and special. However, I now realize that it also created a tremendous amount of pressure as I tried to live up to his expectations, and I'm sure it contributed significantly to my unrelenting drive for self-perfection.

I can also remember that while my asking all those questions was cute when I was a little girl, it became a greater and greater problem as I grew up. I can vividly recall emotionally charged words spewing so venomously from my parents' and teachers' mouths that I would stand there stunned, wondering what I had just done wrong. I remember that every time this happened, I'd feel confused, rejected, stupid, resentful, disappointed, inadequate, and at times even unloved.

I can recall being in second grade when something was said regarding this issue, and then it came up again in junior high and high school. Now that I think about each of these events, I see that while they appeared to be different, they were actually a repeat of the same situation and what I felt at each different age—4, 7, 13, and even 16—all had the same emotional impact. My feelings were deeply hurt, my self-confidence took a nosedive, and the perception I had of myself and my intelligence was greatly diminished. This happened to such an extent that I still—even to this day—revisit these feelings not only in my mind, but also in my body through the aches and pains I experience when I find myself in similar situations.

So there's my story. What's yours? Everybody has one. Some are good and some are awful; some are tragic and some are poignant; some are funny and some are even outrageous. The truth is that we all have at least one good tale that we tell and retell as a way of getting the attention we need or to explain why we feel bad about ourselves. We recount these events to explain why we carry the emotional baggage we do—or for that matter, why we carry the weight we do. We justify why we're afraid to love, heal, change, and succeed and why we have anxieties and other issues. We try to get people to comfort us, feel sorry for us, help us, and even love us.

Interestingly, the stories and the emotional charges we attach to them tend to remain consistent throughout our lives. However, how we use the narratives changes over the course of time. Sometimes they're a means of rationalizing why we stay stuck in the past, and other times they help us avoid doing things we don't want to do. We seduce people into our dramas and traumas so that they, too, can share in our worrying and pain, and we even make others feel guilty for what they did to us or for not helping us.

Then there are the times when how we use our stories changes. Instead of supporting self-limiting and self-defeating behavior, they help us understand why we feel the way we do and uncover why we have self-distorted perceptions. When we think about them in this way, they can help us identify the mental limitations that are holding us back as adults, leading us to believe that we can't accomplish our goals or live our dreams. At this point, our tales serve as powerful positive motivators and catalysts for change. They can also heal when we share them with those who have experienced the same emotional hurts.

I'm sure you can recall stories of persistence, perseverance, determination, fearlessness, and someone having the courage to walk into the dark night of the soul only to come out of the experience enlightened. What about the accounts of battling cancer and winning, and those about overcoming insurmountable obstacles to create a life that we'd all love? In these situations, the telling and retelling of events isn't just appropriate, it's imperative, because they serve as inspiration and offer hope. We all need a daily dose of motivation if we're going to stay positively engaged in life and remain healthy. These are the kinds of stories that touch our hearts and give us courage to keep going when things get tough.

The ones we need to watch out for are those that encourage self-pity, foster victim behavior, and cause us to experience the destructive emotions of hopelessness, helplessness, despair, disappointment, hate, and anger. These accounts don't serve us well because we use them as excuses and they prevent us from manifesting our true potential. They make us feel bad about ourselves and keep us stuck in the patterns of behavior that prevent us from taking a risk or trying something new. These are the plots that feed our fears, leave us emotionally vulnerable, and cause us to compromise who we really are. They make us afraid to express ourselves and share our emotional needs. These are the stories we need to change because they will ultimately surface in our bodies in the form of illness and disease later in life.

Unraveling Our Origins

The development of who we are and what we become is truly an extraordinary process. We enter this world open, naïve, and innocent. Everything we do is new. Life creates joy, awe, wonderment, and excitement; and we find great pleasure in simple accomplishments. As babies, we squeal with delight the first time we hear our voices and discover our laughs, and we spend long periods of time engrossed in watching the movement of our hands and fingers. As toddlers, we're tickled when we pull ourselves up at a table and even more pleased when we take our first step.

We look around to see if anyone is watching, and we learn to be attentive to the expressions on our parents' faces to see if they're excited, too. If they clap and cheer us on we feel good about ourselves and are willing to take more steps until we're walking on our own. On the other hand, if they scold us for touching the table and getting into things now that we're mobile, we experience the confusion of mixed messages. We begin to recognize what makes them happy and what doesn't. However, at this age, while the awareness of what pleases our parents heightens, our focus is still on our needs and getting what we want when we want it. If necessary, we use emotional outbursts as a means of ensuring that this will be the case. Our determination remains undaunted.

The ages from three to six mark a significant change. We enter the socialization phase of life, which means we move from being the center of things to sharing the spotlight with others. As a result, we find ourselves competing for attention and seeking praise, recognition, approval, and acceptance in order to experience love and feel good about ourselves.

Our motivation shifts from our own desires to meeting the needs of other people. We experience time and rules, and we discover that our wishes will only be fulfilled if we learn to become compliant and adapt to the demands of others. Our emotional outbursts are no longer tolerated, and we're admonished when we do the things we did as toddlers. Our emotional reactions begin to mirror those of other people: parents, siblings, day-care providers, and teachers.

Yet even with this adjustment, our inner child still remains curious, undeterred, rebellious, and willing to try new things. An example of this would be our learning to ride a bicycle. The thought of a new bike excites us because it's our initial taste of freedom, independence, and realization that we're in control. The first time we get on the bike, we feel safe because our parents tell us that we have training wheels which will prevent us from falling down. We learn to depend on those wheels to keep us upright and move forward. Then they're removed, and we struggle to find balance and control. We fall down, get up, and try again until we master the art of riding. We don't care about crying when we fall down—and we don't give up. We only tend to get discouraged and become emotionally reactive when someone else tells us that we're not very good, and we learn that crying is bad if we're chastised for it.

The years from 6 to 13 present a whole new myriad of problems and challenges for us because it's the period when we're the most impressionable and emotionally vulnerable to other people's perceptions and opinions, even those of total strangers. As a matter of fact, the majority of the stories we tell and retell as adults originate during this time frame, because this is when we're developing our self-confidence, self-esteem, self-worth, and future self-perceptions. These are the years when conditioning takes its greatest toll on our individuality and self-expression because they're when we make the conscious choice to suppress our inner child. We learn that expressing our emotions or talking about our needs isn't necessarily welcomed, appreciated, embraced, or even appropriate. We begin to form our perceptions of love and the expectations about what we want in our relationships as adults.

These years also find us looking outside our family for the recognition, praise, and acceptance we long for. We need people to like us and tell us we're special, smart, artistic, cheerful, helpful, resourceful, or talented. It's within this time span that our stories start to become our identities. If people tell us that we're smart students, good kids, likable, enjoyable to be around, pretty or handsome, popular, or going to go far in life, then we believe them and create healthy self-perceptions. On the other hand, if we're told that we're dumb, incorrigible, inadequate, troublemakers, poor students, social misfits, unable to make the right choices, or not good enough—or that we'll never amount to anything in life—we believe them and create unhealthy self-perceptions.

The result is that we live up—or down—to those views throughout our entire life. If our perceptions are healthy, so are our stories; and conversely, if they're unhealthy, then so is what we tell ourselves. However, no matter how wonderful our childhood and how positive our stories, everyone has at least one thread that they struggle with and recount over and over when they're feeling bad about themselves. Right or wrong, fair or unfair, it's this time in our lives when other people's expectations and their own unhealthy narratives impact us the most and become the self-fulfilling prophesies of our adulthood.

Looking at how conditioning impacts us and forms our stories, it's easy to understand why we struggle in life and suffer the way we do, and why these tales have such a great impact on our health. It's easy to understand how every experience, situation, and fable that surfaced during this time becomes the source of the thoughts we create and recreate as adults. They perpetuate ideas, feed self-perceptions, and influence how we view our outer world. These become thoughts that determine how we cope with our life and deal with adversity—what's responsible for developing the attitudes, beliefs, habits, and comfort zones that encourage us to tell and retell the same old stories.

Then on top of all of those thoughts there are our interactions with other people—our loves and hates, our emotional wounds and hurts, our joys and disappointments, and our successes and failures. They, too, are all there in the form of stories and are encoded in our mind and body. They're just waiting for the right time, place, and opportunity to be told and retold either verbally or physically.

Digging Deeper Into Our Storytelling Coffers

The developmental process of who we are and what we become isn't intended to be static, void of change, free of challenges, safe, or even necessarily comfortable. It's meant to be a dynamic evolutionary process whereby the mind, body, and soul learn how to coexist in the physical world and where each learns how to communicate effectively with the others. This should be a process where the experiences of life and interactions with people serve as catalysts for change so that we may discover who we really are and find meaning in our journeys. It's a developmental process where the focus isn't on the *whats,* but rather on the *whys* of life. For example, *why* do we think and act in certain ways, *why* do we make the choices we do, and *why* do we become ill? *Why* do we have the stories we do, and *why* do we hang on to them even when they aren't in our best interest?

If we're to truly find the answers to the *why* questions, then we're going to have to look beyond the obvious story contributors of conditioning and social pressures and dig deeper. We're going to have to look at the underlying sources such as personality, cultural beliefs, the mother/child relationship, and religion. Because these, too, determine the kinds of narratives we create.

Personality

Personality is without a doubt one of the most significant of all the contributors because it controls why we think and act the way we do, determines why we make choices, and is the single strongest influence over the chemical dialogue between the mind and body. Thus, it controls why we become stressed, why pressure affects us the way it does, why we tend to stay chronically anxious, and why we become ill—stress being the common denominator behind illness and disease. Personality also establishes the boundaries by which we conduct our lives and is the organizing principle that impacts every aspect of our being: mentally, emotionally, physically, and spiritually.

The personality as a whole consists of two aspects: 1) characteristics, and 2) traits. Each of these tends to form its own stories. The ones created by characteristics are representative of learned behavior and mirror our conditioning. Consequently, they reflect the influence other people had over us and exemplify those outside perspectives and opinions. They also tend to have greater negative emotional charges to them since they represent how we compromised who we are in order to fit in and be liked and loved. They seem to be the stories that foster self-pity and create many of the struggles we experience as adults.

Characteristics are referred to as the false personality and are responsible for:

- Creating habits, comfort zones, limiting thoughts, and the distorted perceptions we have of ourselves

- Engendering limiting thoughts, attitudes, and beliefs that encumber personal growth and inhibit the healing process

- Suppressing emotions, individuality, and the expression of our uniqueness

- Causing us to make decisions for other people's reasons and not our own, thus compromising our core values and principles

- Keeping us stuck in thought and behavioral patterns that encourage the repetition of the dramas and traumas created by our stories

Traits, on the other hand, represent our true personality, because they're inherent. In other words, they form the intrinsic neurological hardwiring of the brain that oversees how we gather and process information and how we make decisions. They also govern how we respond internally to external stimuli. Consequently, the stories that traits create are in alignment with our inner nature and are void of personal compromise. They tend to be charged with positive emotions and act as the motivators for changing thoughts and behavior created by our conditioning. They establish our core values and principles and reflect our authentic self. In times of stress, they bring us back to a place of calmness both in our mind and in the chemistry of the body.

Traits are responsible for:

- Creating consistent and predictable patterns of behavior in alignment with our basic needs

- Establishing how we perceive our outer world and experiences and how we cope in life

- Helping us discern our truth from that of other people, thus allowing us to make decisions in alignment with our needs rather than theirs

- Allowing us to be emotionally sensitive without going too far and rational without becoming irrational

- Facilitating the changes necessary to express our authenticity and function within our strengths, thus freeing us from our self-limiting stories

If we are to understand *why* we become unwell and how our stories contribute to the formation of illness, we must begin by learning more about our personality and its inherent needs. Only then will we come to realize the important role it plays in health. It's the only way to understand how compromising our personality traits increases our susceptibility to neurological disorders such as headaches, Parkinson's disease, dementia, multiple sclerosis, and peripheral neuropathy.

Cultural Beliefs

The impact cultural beliefs have on the stories we develop begins the day we're born and continues to unfold throughout childhood, adolescence, adulthood, and even old age. However, these tales are different from the ones we create as a result of our everyday experiences. They're steeped in cultural traditions and represent the beliefs and patterns of many generations. They tell the world how to identify and interact with us, and unfortunately, they're also responsible for prejudices that cause a tremendous amount of suffering and pain.

These beliefs dictate how we live our lives all the way from the dishes we eat to how our foods are prepared, from our sense of responsibility to our usage of money, and from educational expectations to practicing religions. Culturally based stories are predetermined by our ethnic origin and are cast in concrete. They create nonnegotiable rules that govern our behavior, even though we may rebel against them as children. They're deeply steeped in our psyche and steer us toward forming relationships with those who share the same roots, encouraging us to stay within our ethnic lineage. The benefit is that we'll be spared the rejection and conflict that occurs when trying to blend different cultural beliefs.

Such stories ensure the preservation of ancestral traditions and perpetuate the fundamental philosophies of the culture. For example, if your heritage requires the presence of the father in the birthing process and views it as his role to care for and raise the children, then it's your responsibility to carry on those traditions by creating a lifestyle that accommodates them. To do anything less would be disrespectful. In this case, your cultural beliefs focus on the male, thus creating patriarchal stories that support his importance and downplay the role of the female.

However, what about the cultures that believe only women should be a part of the birthing process and that see it as the role of the female to care for and raise the children? In this case, the male will be less valued. The stories will be matriarchal, as will the customs and traditions.

Again, as long as we stay within our cultural roots, there won't be a problem. However, if we create a relationship with someone who shares different beliefs and sees the roles of males and females differently, then there are going to be basic philosophical differences. Those will create an entirely different set of stories.

This has an impact on our health because the tension created when different cultural philosophies clash shows up in the form of allergies, depression, addictions, and post-traumatic stress disorder and in an overall weakening of the immune system. Such strain causes the mind and body to be at odds with each other, which makes both weary of the struggle.

The Mother/Child Relationship

The relationship between a mother and her child is pivotal in determining the kinds of stories we create about love and relationships. This is because of the strong inherent emotional bonds we have with our mothers and how their affection impacts our self-perception, self-worth, and self-esteem. It establishes very early on how we will care for others in the future. If our interactions with our mothers were tender and included a lot of touching and positive displays of love, then our perception of the emotion will share these same qualities. On the other hand, if they rejected us, refused to touch us or acknowledge our presence, or resented the fact that we disrupted their lives, then *that* will be our story of love.

In either case, our relationships with them determine how we interact with others, the quality of our connections, the kinds of people we'll be attracted to, the expectations we bring to those unions, and the perception we have of ourselves in relationships. Without the love, nurturing, stimulation, and protection of our mothers, not only would our survival be questionable, so would our degree of emotional and mental stability.

The bonds between mother and child actually begin in the womb, and many of the psychological responses we express throughout our lives reflect maternal responses during the pregnancy gestation period. In an article written by Dr. Paul Pearsall, he tells of an experiment conducted by the United States Army Intelligence and Security Command that shows the intimate connection we have with our mothers and how their emotional reactions to external situations become imprinted in the babies' cells while still in the womb and how, once the babies are born, those same emotional reactions are expressed through the infants' cellular activity.

Here's how the experiment went: It began with a selection of pregnant women who were subjected to highly stressful lifestyles, meaning that they feared for their survival and that of their children, and they lived in undesirable environments where safety was a daily concern. After the children were born and before they were sent home, saliva was removed from the children and put in test tubes.

The mothers and children were then separated, as were the test tubes of the children's saliva. The mothers were sent to one part of the hospital, and the saliva to another; the children remained in the safety and security of the nursery. The mothers were then subjected to disturbing and traumatic pictures and sounds that replicated their external surroundings while they were pregnant. As the women reacted emotionally, a polygraph recorded any changes that occurred in them and in the cells of the children's saliva. They found that the greater the mothers' emotional reactions, the stronger the excitations of the cells in the test tube.

The conclusion drawn from this experiment was that the cells of the children seemed to remember the mothers' emotional reactions to their external surroundings even while in the womb, and those memories were so embedded in the children's psyches that they caused the cells in the saliva to react with the same intensity and excitation as the mothers. This meant there must be an inherent connection between mothers and children that makes it possible for them to share the same emotional recollections and reactions.

This certainly puts a different twist on the statement: "Oh no, I'm becoming my mother." The fact is that we *are,* in the sense that we share many of the same emotional memories.

Religion

While we may not consider religion to be a contributor to our stories, it really is, and for many of the same reasons that cultural beliefs are. The stories created as the result of religious tenets are steeped in ancient traditions. They seek to preserve fundamental notions and the codes of conduct that dictate how we live our lives, and in some cases may even determine who we marry.

When I was doing my research in preparation for receiving my doctorate in religious philosophy, I learned that while appearing different, religions share many of the same attributes. They have basic messages intended to offer direction and guidance, and they possess fundamental principles and truths founded in their beliefs. Their messages speak of some connection with a Creator, even though that being is called different names. Their teachings refer to acceptable and unacceptable behavior, and all offer the opportunity for those who follow their wisdom to redeem themselves, thus creating the quality of life they desire.

This is the case unless someone is an atheist or agnostic, which interestingly is a different form of doctrine per se.

There are still fundamental principles and codes of conduct that dictate what people believe and how they should live. The only missing component is the worshipping of a deity.

However, as I delved deeper into the doctrines offered by a variety of different faiths, I discovered that religions—including those that didn't worship a deity—could be separated into two categories: 1) those that engage us emotionally, and 2) those that engage us mentally. And interestingly, it didn't seem to make a difference whether the teachings were steeped in Eastern or Western traditions. The same held true. This discovery alone helped me understand why we create the stories we do around religion and how they affect not only the perceptions we have of ourselves and the quality of our lives, but also our health.

Take, for example, the difference between suffering and struggling. Religions whose messages engage us emotionally focus on anguish, teaching that it's an affliction of the human condition and that it's natural for us to endure things the way we do. They offer the idea that suffering is the result of engaging in behavior that isn't in alignment with the desires of the Creator. It's brought about due to ignorance or misperception and is linked to unacceptable attitudes and beliefs.

These religions also acknowledge that suffering serves a purpose, for it's a powerful motivator for those seeking to find meaning in their lives and gain a deeper understanding of their place in the world. These traditions don't see it as shameful to experience difficulty. Instead they see it as a noble act that helps cleanse the impurities of human action and aids us in discovering our spiritual nature. Their writings use emotionally charged words to describe human trauma, such as *pain, abandonment, loneliness, despair, hopeless,* and *helpless.* These terms not only show up in our stories, but also in our bodies in the form of chronic neck and shoulder pain and illnesses such as asthma, diabetes, fibromyalgia, and heart disease.

On the other hand, religions whose messages engage us mentally focus on the struggles of life and teach that conflict is the result of thoughts and patterns of thinking that separate our head from our heart, and both of these from our divine nature. Their teachings offer guidance and direction in mental management and encourage reflecting on our challenges so that we may find ways to free ourselves from the conditioning and obsessions of the mind. They see value in struggling, because they believe it's the vehicle that can help us recognize that something needs to change. However, they don't see any merit in suffering.

Their teachings focus on the power of the mind and teach us that what we think, we become. Their guidance shows us how to heighten our inner awareness so that we may listen to our internal dialogue and observe our behavior. They help us reframe negative self-talk into positive words. They tell us that we alone can change what causes us to be at odds with ourselves and prevents us from expressing our full potential. These religions use words such as *limitations, perceptions, consciousness, disempowering, unresolved,* and *distortion* and phrases such *as mentally paralyzed, wake-up call,* and *out of control.*

The result is that their stories are as different from the tales of suffering as the behaviors they create. If we allow ourselves to constantly strive against everything, then we will always be at odds with ourselves. Such struggle weakens the immune system and can lead to autoimmune disorders such as chronic infections, chronic fatigue syndrome, and Hashimoto's thyroiditis. It can also contribute to various kinds of arthritis, such as rheumatoid arthritis and osteoarthritis, and even factor into kidney disease, stroke, and degenerative blood diseases such as multiple myeloma.

Stories . . . Life's Gifts

If we were to look at our stories as a chronological history of our lives, we'd begin to gain a different appreciation for them. Instead of seeing them as just one darn thing after another and looking through the eyes of suffering and struggle, we'd understand that they're the record keepers of our lives. We would see them as mileposts highlighting our turning points, benchmarks in the evolution of our personal growth and spiritual development.

When we look at our stories from this perspective, it's easy to see how every item in our storytelling coffers serves a purpose and why, taken together, they truly are life's gifts. After all, they represent every challenge we've faced, every fear we've conquered, every success we've experienced, every dream we've manifested, and every obstacle we've overcome—even when we didn't think we could. They reflect every role we've played throughout our lives and all of the identities we've created as the result of our childhood, adolescence, and even adulthood. All of these tales, whether positive or negative, are gifts in some way because they've all been instrumental in helping us gain a greater understanding of who we are. They've shown us what we're capable of achieving.

They reveal the core themes of our lives and illustrate that no matter how large the problem, there's always a solution, and within every challenge there are buried gifts. We may shift our perception or change in some other way, discover alternative solutions and possibilities, learn to let go, and heal ourselves. They show us that it's the stories with the strongest emotional charges that offer the greatest opportunity for personal growth, and through their metaphors they demonstrate how our core themes are impacting both our life and our health.

They also created the rose-colored glasses we put on as children. Examining what we tell ourselves reveals how wearing those glasses has become so comfortable that they've distorted our perceptions of the outer world, which has an impact on how we interact with others. These stories uncover how we've embraced the truths of others and how those have caused us to make ourselves small and act as if we aren't important.

The most important gift of our stories is that they help us discern our thoughts from those of other people. We find out how those ideas aren't in alignment with our soul's intentions. They do so by making us feel uncomfortable, creating the awareness that we're compromising ourselves and selling ourselves short. They show us how our mythology affects our biology through the tension, stress, emotional strain, aches, and pains we feel when we find ourselves telling and retelling a story that no longer serves us well. Carl Jung said, "Every human being had a story, or to put (it) in its most evolved form, a myth of its own."

Changing the Stories

If our stories are such an integral part of who we are, then how do we change them without losing our sense of identity? How do we stop the powerful hold they have over us, moving beyond the patterns of thinking and behavior that hold us back? How do we rid ourselves of the core themes created by our conditioning and other people's perceptions and opinions? And finally, how do we transform the stories that encourage us to stay afraid, follow the path of least resistance, and play it safe, or cause us to try to march to the same drummer as everyone else—even when we're out of step?

We begin to make those changes by looking at our lives and asking ourselves if the stories we're telling over and over are creating the environment we need to support our inner needs each day. Are they having an impact on the quality of life we desire? We can then recognize that we alone determine the landscape of our outer world, for we are both the painter and the canvas. We must remember that our stories shouldn't control us. We should direct them, for their purpose is to serve as catalysts for change. Then we can recognize how thoughts, emotions, attitudes, and beliefs create the behavior we live every day and flavor our experiences.

By reminding ourselves that everything manifesting in our outer world began as a single thought, we can learn how to manage these patterns. We come to understand that the more time we spend with a thought, the stronger the emotions we attach to it. The more intense our emotions, the greater the hold it has over us and the more likely we are to empower it by amplifying it with other ideas that then turn into our stories.

We'll start living in the present moment because that's the only way we'll be aware of the choices we're making and can hear the stories we're telling. If they don't bring passion and joy to our lives, then we can willfully and justifiably change them.

Don't allow yourself to be held prisoner by your stories—they may well rob you of the life and health you desire.

They can distort your perceptions, cause you to identify with your illnesses, and hold you hostage in an unhealthy body. Remember, only you hold the keys that can free you from limiting thoughts and can change your stories. Only you can heal yourself.

What are you waiting for?

CHAPTER 5

It's All about Perceptions

The following story illustrates the strength of perceptions. Alice came to me for a medical intuitive reading because she was dissatisfied with herself, her life, and the people in it. Everything was a struggle, a crisis, and an emotional trauma. She admitted that she was always angry and disappointed and lived in constant fear that something bad was going to happen. Even when she did something that she said she enjoyed, such as sewing, which used to be a real passion of hers, she found that she didn't get any pleasure from it. Nor did she feel fulfilled when she finished a project.

She complained that things were never good enough no matter how hard she tried, and she never seemed to please people, even though her perception was that she was always doing things for others and neglecting herself. She worried constantly and most of the time wasn't even sure what she was so anxious about. All she knew was that her life wasn't what she wanted it to be. She felt as though there was always a dark cloud hanging over her that made her feel overshadowed by low-grade anxiety that never seemed to go away—it would even wake her up in the middle of the night.

Alice was unwilling to open up emotionally to the people in her life because she was afraid they'd find out that she wasn't as strong as she'd led them to believe. She worried that they'd be disappointed in her or—worse yet—would leave her. So she buried her anger, suppressed her emotions, continued to put the needs of others before her own, and suffered silently when all she wanted was to feel loved and have people care for her the way she did for them.

If this was what she really wanted, then why was she so afraid to open up? It's because of her story and the anger she'd let build up around it. The tale had become bigger than life and distorted her self-perception so significantly that she believed any display of emotions would be perceived as a character flaw.

But then something happened: Her story impacted her health. Alice had an emotional breakdown and ended up having to spend time in a recovery center for severe depression. In her mind, she blamed the people in her life for causing this and decided that the best thing to do was to separate herself from them emotionally. Once she made this break in her mind, she found that she liked being away from their demands. She enjoyed being around individuals who understood her misery, who cared about her, who listened, and who had experienced the same thing. For the first time in her life, she was told that it was okay to feel what she did, to tell her story, and to bring to the surface the deep emotional hurts she'd buried inside. Interestingly, anytime the physicians suggested that she could go home, she had a relapse.

After awhile, Alice was diagnosed with manic-depressive illness, and it immediately changed her. At that point, she could go home because she could explain to people why she felt the way she did. Being labeled gave her a new perception of herself, as well as a new story. She began to use the illness as her identity and embraced it in a way that allowed it to control her rather than the other way around.

She was put on one medication after another in an attempt to find something that would offer her the emotional stability that she claimed she wanted. Her prescription dosages were constantly being increased because she believed they weren't helping anymore. Then she would blame the physicians for not getting it right and would take herself off all drugs . . . and her anger would build up again. However, rather than suppressing her emotions as she did before, she'd burst into a tirade that would leave those around her wondering what hit them. The people in her life would back away and avoid her for the fear of triggering one of her outbursts. Immediately following such an episode, she'd blame her illness and the doctors for not making her well—but she knew exactly what she was doing.

She was using her illness to get the attention she wanted, as well as making it the vehicle to express her emotions. Her perception was that her condition was a good thing because it gave her what she needed. So when I suggested looking for ways to remove the stories and perceptions behind her diagnosis, she really wasn't interested. She preferred to stay immersed in her own private world of self-indulged dysfunction.

The Mythology/Biology Connection

Linking the stories of our lives with the health of the body isn't a new concept. The ancient physicians and metaphysicians of Egypt, Greece, and China would use this connection to help them understand the roots behind a person's illness and direct them in the healing process. Even Hippocrates turned to the mythology/biology connection to help him diagnose and treat illness. He believed: *As a person thinketh, so shall he be.* Consequently, he evaluated a person's mental state to help understand the physical.

Hippocrates held that the mind and body would *imitate* and *imprint* each other, so what affected one had an impact on the other. Because of this belief, he saw the healing process consisting of two phases. Phase 1 required changing the current mental state, because without doing so the mind would return to its old patterns of thinking, behavior would continue to support unhealthy lifestyle choices and habits, and the body would maintain its chronic physical infirmities. Phase 2 involved creating a new mental state. In doing so, there would be new choices and behaviors and a different lifestyle—one conducive to the healing of both the mind and the body. Over and over again, his work revealed the importance of a healthy mental condition for both healing and sustaining good health.

Sigmund Freud also understood the importance of a healthy mental state and used the mythology/biology connection in his approach to understanding why we become ill. He believed that by uncovering the stories buried deeply within the human psyche, the body would respond favorably. Consequently, he created a "talking cure" that required people to tell and retell their stories, speaking about their pasts as a means of releasing the emotional hurts responsible for their unhealthy mental state. Freud believed that when the stories were left internalized, they'd fester and build on themselves, much like a bacterial infection. As a result, his approach to healing was to bring the tales to the surface so that the mind/body connection could help heal each function. Yet if this were truly the case then we should all be well, for it's a natural part of human nature to recount our stories.

While Freud's approach is certainly sound in concept and does offer some relief, it doesn't ensure the stories or the emotional wounds will go away—even after years of therapy. Why not? There are two underlying factors. The first is that it doesn't address how we use the narratives and the purpose they serve. Let me explain. Haven't you found that the more you talk about your troubles, the unhappier you get . . . and the worse you feel, the more you find yourself wanting to surround yourself with people who also are down? It's that old self-fulfilling prophecy syndrome.

We use our story of unhappiness to justify staying upset, and we support this by hanging around people who are in the same state. After all, if they're unhappy then there isn't anything wrong with us if we are, too. Here's another example: What about the tales of how we've been hurt by those who said they cared for us? Haven't you found that the more you talk about those grievances, the tighter their grip? Doesn't dwelling on them feed your fear of relationships? In this case, we use our stories to explain why we're afraid to love and why we avoid any situations that may rekindle those old wounds. And if we ever do enter into another relationship, we use these same yarns to explain our unhealthy codependency. In both of these situations, the stories are used to protect us.

The second factor regarding why the talking cure doesn't always work is because other people can't make what we tell ourselves go away. All they can do is lend a sympathetic ear and—in the case of therapists—share their expertise. They can only help us if we're willing to help ourselves. In other words, we have to do it on our own for our reasons. It's up to us to shift the perceptions we have and to let go of the identities they create.

This means that at some point we're going to have to stop telling and retelling the stories, especially those that are charged with self-pity, because rather than being a solution, they're compounding the problem. Instead of liberating us from the past, they're keeping us trapped in what's familiar. As a result, our history dictates our future, and we find ourselves perpetuating an insidious storytelling cycle that could eventually surface in the body in the form of diabetes, heart disease, chronic fatigue, autoimmune disorders, and even certain cancers.

What we're learning from the mythology/biology connection is that if a person *believes* their illness is serving a purpose, *feels* that it's fulfilling a deep emotional need, and *owns* it by personalizing and identifying with it, then they *become* their illness. We're learning that it's all about *perceptions.*

Perceptions . . . Life's Baggage

A perception is a combination of thoughts, emotions, attitudes, and beliefs that form a mental state or a state of consciousness. When repeated, they become the truths that color our view of the world. They influence our behavior, establish our core themes, affect the quality of our lives, influence our interactions with other people, decide how we cope with life's challenges, and have a major impact on our overall health and well-being. Perceptions are the basis of our stories and significantly determine the ones we consistently tell and retell. Think of them as life's baggage, for they hold within them the contents of everything that happens to us from childhood to adulthood.

If we use the metaphor "Life's a journey," we begin to understand why we have the baggage we do and how we've accumulated its contents. It's there because of the travel—we aren't born with it. We actually come into this world with a metaphoric carrying case, the *mind,* that's designed to hold all of our experiences. It already comes equipped with personality traits to tell us how to think and get where we want to go. It holds the sacred agreement we have with ourselves, which is to bring our soul's intentions into physical expression through our thoughts, words, and actions. However, the mind doesn't contain fear, pain, or suffering at birth. These emotions are added as a result of our conditioning and when we accept and speak other people's truths as if they were our own. It's at this point that the carrying case becomes baggage and perceptions misalign with our soul's intentions.

Some people may not agree with this because they've been conditioned to believe that we're born already laden with karma, suffering, anger, guilt, disappointment, and despair. Karma, in that context, refers to behavior and unfinished business in this life and previous lives that somehow predetermines a destiny and prevents them from exercising free will. Consequently, their perception is that they can't find happiness or live joyful lives until they rid themselves of that karma—nor can they heal themselves. This leads them to believe that the more they suffer and the harder they work, the greater the chances that they can create the life and health they desire.

Rarely is there good karma in this world view—only bad. However, for some there may be an upside. Bad karma can be blamed for what happens and why we aren't able to be in control, and it can excuse bad behavior. This perception also explains why some people will just accept illness and are willing to relegate the healing process to someone else rather than believing that they can do something themselves.

Going back to the metaphor "Life's a journey," we see that we begin with a carrying case. Then as we go along, we're constantly adding thoughts, throwing in some emotions to support them, and carefully packing in some attitudes just in case something comes along that challenges our perceptions. Thinking that we have everything, we're ready to close the baggage and move forward.

Then we suddenly remember that we've forgotten our beliefs. Without them, we won't be able to tell if the truths that are driving how we live belong to us or someone else. We're pleased with ourselves for remembering them and relieved to have them with us because we know deep inside that they'll keep us safe in our comfort zones and patterns of habitual behavior. We can always count on them to explain why we don't or can't overcome our fears. Then our mind tells us that we're ready to go on because our baggage is full of everything we need to fit into our societal and familial structures.

However, in the background we can hear this little voice—our soul's voice—wanting to know if we really need all that. It wonders why we're not speaking our own truths and why we haven't packed any happiness, joy, fun, play, or self-love. It asks, "If you haven't packed any of these things, how will you change your perceptions, find the pleasures of life, or experience the excitement and wonder that happens when you try something new—such as creating a new thought, letting go of an old hurt, or marching to your own drummer? How will you discover what you're capable of achieving? How will you create a life that's in alignment with your soul's purpose? Most important, how will you heal yourself?"

It asks us to go back to the beginning of our journey, when we didn't have any baggage and all we possessed was a carrying case lightly filled with thoughts and emotions. There weren't any attitudes or beliefs to weigh us down, nor were there any perceptions to hold us back. It reminds us of how free we felt; how spontaneous, flexible, and adaptable we were; and how easy it was to go with the flow. It asks us to remember how every day was an adventure and each experience offered us the opportunity to learn, grow, and experience something new. It brings up how we were like a kid in a candy store believing we could have it all and pursuing what we believed with enthusiasm and determination.

This voice also points out how we've changed throughout the years. The older we get, the heavier our baggage becomes, until one day we reach a point where it's so overstuffed that we aren't able to close it. It's so heavy that we can't carry it anymore. It explains that if we continue to do this, our mind will become exhausted from the stress, and we'll find ourselves experiencing indecisiveness and confusion. This voice reminds us of how our body suffers from the stress of lifting, packing, and repacking the same old perceptions and dragging them around with us every day until our back hurts, our feet are tired and achy, and our immune system is weary and weakened, increasing our susceptibility to illness. It says that it's because of baggage that we forget who we are and allow the perceptions of others to misalign us with our soul's purpose.

Our soul's voice asks us to remember that the key to good health begins by evaluating our views and acting on them before they become our baggage. It suggests that the best way to start the healing process is by looking at our perceptions of illness because they will determine how we'll relate to and identify with the condition, and what kinds of treatments we'll seek. It will also influence our commitment to participate in the healing process, meaning whether we'll look to others to make things better or if we're willing to do so ourselves.

The Perceptions of Illness

There are basically four fundamental perceptions of illness:

1. Mental: The mind is aware that there's something wrong with the body, but it's not identifiable.

2. Physical: The body produces a definable illness that can be objectively identified through symptoms or tests.

3. Psychological: Illness is perceived as a breakdown between the mind/body connection; it addresses how the mental state is affecting the physical.

4. Psychospiritual: Illness is assessed holistically and identified as a transpersonal crisis of the soul, mind, and body; it considers the breakdown in how each communicates, works, and supports the others, thus affecting the health and well-being of all.

Unfortunately, this fourth perception of illness isn't usually taken into consideration when we're experiencing minor aches and pains. It only comes into play when we're diagnosed with something life threatening, and even then allopathic medicine doesn't place value on it because the establishment doesn't understand it or its healing qualities. This is primarily because of the immeasurable qualities associated with it, meaning how we measure the soul's intentions—or for that matter, the soul and its energetic nature—in blind studies. How do we quantify the physiological wear and tear caused by thoughts, emotions, stories, and other baggage? The truth is that we can't, especially if we continue to look at illness as the result of external factors and only treat the body.

The Mental Perception of Illness

It's this perception of illness that drives most people to seek medical attention because the mind is aware that something's wrong when we don't feel well or our body hurts. As a result, we obsess over the physical symptoms and fixate on trying to identify the problem until we create enough stress and concern that we're forced to take action. Then when we do seek help, the only thing the mind is interested in is having a doctor or other health-care practitioner identify the issue and offer a quick physical fix. The primary focus is understanding what's happening in the body and finding out how long it will take to restore it to good health.

If people view illness this way, they'll most likely be open to any form of medication that eases the discomfort, whether it's natural, pharmaceutical, potentially addictive, or has a risk of long-term side effects. Their concern, and that of their mind, is to feel better and to make the pain go away.

Unfortunately, if folks have a mental perception of illness, a sizable percentage who see a doctor will leave without an explanation or diagnosis because there's no identifiable pathology. When this happens, both the patients and doctors will be frustrated. In addition, there's also the cost both in time and money for running diagnostic tests that produce nothing and engaging in treatment options for a condition that doesn't exist. At this point, the mind doesn't know where to get its answers nor can the people figure out what the next steps should be. Without a diagnosis, they're forced to accept that there's nothing to be done because no one knows what's wrong. They must learn to live with their discomfort, adjusting their lifestyle and accepting whatever is needed to manage the pain.

It's important to remember that the mental perception of illness focuses solely on the functioning of the body—nothing more. Its primary objective is to create a heightened state of awareness that something's wrong and to draw attention to the physical area where the breakdown is occurring. The mind accomplishes this by increasing the level of pain receptors released in the brain and directing them to the part of the body that's being compromised. If the mind does its job well, we take action, because it becomes impossible to think about anything else.

The Physical Perception of Illness

The physical perception is a completely different story because there's an actual diagnosable illness that's specifically affecting the body. However, in many cases—such as the early stages of cancer, heart disease, and diabetes—we may not be aware there's anything wrong because we're not experiencing symptoms that would drive us to seek help. In this situation, the issue is generally found through routine diagnostic testing, which is a good news/bad news scenario.

The good news is that by being diligent in getting regular checkups and routine tests, the problem can be discovered early enough that it can be treated successfully. The bad news is that when there are no physical symptoms, we may be blindsided by the diagnosis and may be less inclined to believe it's true. When this occurs, it isn't unusual for us to deny we have an illness, challenge the diagnosis, question the competency of the doctor, or reject any suggestion of treatment until the mind fully grasps what it's dealing with. Unfortunately, while it deals with the denial and tries to gain understanding, the condition may progress to the point where there are fewer treatment options.

The physical perception believes that illness is the result of external factors such as viruses, bacterial infections, chemical exposure, environmental contaminants, physical injury or trauma, or biological predispositions such as family history. It's focused on how the structure of the body is being affected and seeks to identify specifically what caused the breakdown in the first place and to what extent the body has been affected. Is the trouble isolated in one area or are others being affected also?

From this standpoint, we're made up of individualized parts such as organs, glands, and a variety of different systems. The body isn't seen holistically. Therefore, the preferred treatment is removing or repairing the affected parts and—if needed—using chemical treatments such as chemotherapy, insulin injections, or pharmaceuticals. As with the mental perception, the physical view is also focused on restoring the body to where it was before it became ill, even if that means potentially compromising another part in the process.

The Psychological Perception of Illness

Our third perception of illness, the psychological one, occurs when we're concerned with our mental state and are trying to understand if it's affecting the physical. We look at the contributors such as lack of sleep, fatigue, stress, emotional troubles, loss of appetite, and an overall sense of not feeling well. We consider health and illness to be a continuum and think that our mental disposition is the only difference between feeling good and not being well.

Even though this perception of illness is psychological in nature, it contributes significantly to our seeking medical attention. It can produce physical symptoms such as muscle tension, pain, heart palpitations, and shortness of breath—signs alerting the mind that something is wrong, even though a doctor may not detect any abnormality. Physicians refer to this as the *worry perception,* meaning that the illnesses it produces are more in the head than the body.

Let me explain: If we're stressed, anxious, or worried, then we're more apt to become preoccupied with our aches and pains and fixate on them to the point that we'll begin to perceive them as indicators that something more serious is wrong. The risk is that we potentially create an imagined condition that could surface as a real one in the future. Worse yet, the illusory problem could become so real that we build a relationship with it to the point of creating sick behavior. This perception of illness reveals just how powerful the mind is, its capability of creating a medical crisis when none exists, and how it can easily make a mountain out of a molehill.

This perception defines illness in terms of behavior, and it reveals how behavioral patterns can influence the well-being of our bodies. An example of this is feeling stuck because we're afraid to make a change, which might surface as constipation or foot problems. Another example might be submissive or victim conduct as a result of being subjected to a controlling, domineering, or abusive relationship. Such circumstances could create a feeling of helplessness which might surface as asthma; they could also lead to a fear of speaking up, which could then appear in the body as a thyroid or throat issue.

Looking at illness from this perception makes it easy to see how negative situations create detrimental thoughts, emotions, attitudes, and beliefs. They can result in an unfavorable mental state that not only affects our behavior, but also how we feel about ourselves, thus creating those vague, intermittent, and difficult-to-diagnose symptoms that leave us and our doctors wondering what's going on.

If this perception of illness is to be addressed properly, the process must include evaluating a person's mental state, identifying patterns of behavior that may ultimately impact the body, and offering cognitive and behavioral modification techniques that will empower the individual to make the necessary changes.

The Psychospiritual Perception of Illness

Our psychospiritual perception is, without a doubt, the most important for healing ourselves because it allows us to see illness holistically. It lets us consider every other perception discussed in this chapter and seek to understand all of their hidden contributors. It forces us to look beyond the physical qualities of the mind/body connection and takes into account the soul's intentions. Consequently, we don't see being sick as merely a breakdown functionally or structurally, but more as a transpersonal crisis indicating that the problem is likely to be both psychological and spiritual.

In this perception of illness, we view the soul, mind, and body as being one and connected by energy. Therefore a disruption to any one of these affects all of them. We seek to identify the obstacles that are preventing the soul's intentions from finding expression through our thoughts, words, actions, and relationships. We want to understand what self-limiting stories and baggage are causing us to compromise who we are and feel bad about ourselves, thus affecting our body. Within this perception of illness, we're concerned with uncovering all of the hidden meanings because we know that without doing so, healing isn't possible.

This viewpoint doesn't define our condition through aches and pains or by identifiable disorders. Instead, it looks at how being unwell impacts our quality of life. We see any problems more as opportunities for reevaluating and transforming the thoughts and emotional patterns responsible for preventing us from having the health we desire. By creating a transpersonal crisis, we're forced to look beyond the obviousness of the body's symptoms and let go of the mental fixations associated with pain. We're required to delve deeper into our storytelling coffers and uncover all of the factors responsible for creating our unhealthy mental state.

This perception enables us to see pain, discomfort, tension, and stress as barometers indicating how much we've compromised our true selves in order to fit into our societal and familial structures, to get ahead, or to be accepted. It views illness as a sign of just how significant the disconnection is among the soul, mind, and body. It reminds us of the need to create our lifestyle around our health rather than vice versa.

Whereas the mind's perception of illness speaks through symptoms, the physical perception speaks through diagnosis, and the psychological perception speaks through behavior, the psychospiritual perception of illness uses metaphors. Here are some examples:

- "Stop dragging your feet" indicates the need to take the steps toward changing what you know you must. This metaphor manifests psychologically as a fear of the unknown, which can be expressed physically as pain and disorders in the feet, ankles, and lower back.

- "It's all in your head" reveals the need to change the thoughts responsible for creating the mental limitations you believe are holding you back. This metaphor manifests psychologically in behavior—such as being overly self-critical or indecisive and taking life too seriously—which then can appear physically as headaches, shoulder and neck muscle tension, and upper spinal disorders.

- "Life's hard" indicates the need to stop and reevaluate your lifestyle. This metaphor manifests psychologically as the fear of change, which show up physically as heart disease, kidney stones, rheumatoid arthritis, and fibromyalgia.

Our psychospiritual perception of illness doesn't have us looking for quick fixes or instant relief through medications; nor does it support emotional avoidance or engaging in passive behavior. Instead, it encourages the expression of stories, negative emotions, and perceptions so that we can bring them to the surface and see how much they've impacted our lives. It views strong negative emotions such as fear, anger, hate, and rage as indicators of how much time and energy we've invested in perpetuating something that compromises who we are. The expression of grief is a natural part of the healing process and a means of letting go of the emotional charges buried deep within our psyche. Self-forgiveness is the only way to heal the disconnection of the soul, mind, and body; it allows us to heal ourselves on all levels.

The value of this perception is that it compels us to take action and forces us to make the changes necessary to heal the breakdown. It requires us to participate in the process rather than abdicating responsibility for our health and well-being. The psychospiritual approach values remembering what it feels like to be healthy—where everything is better than it was before we became ill.

The Only Perception that Really Matters

As we saw in the case of Alice at the beginning of this chapter, the only perception that mattered was hers. It didn't make any difference what her physicians thought or what their conclusions were. She embraced her illness, owned it, identified with it, and used it to her advantage. She developed such a positive psychological relationship with it that she was determined to perpetuate it.

Likewise, the only perception of illness that matters is our own. It's the only one that will determine the relationship we'll develop with our condition, the types of treatments we'll be receptive to trying, our tolerance for dealing with its impact on our life, and the degree of our participation in the healing process. Our outlook will drive whether we'll seek instant relief and a doctor to fix us or whether we're willing to repair ourselves. It will determine whether we're willing to look deeper than the physical symptoms and diagnoses to uncover the hidden meanings behind the illness, and if we're willing to transform those latent messages by releasing their emotional charges.

I encourage you to take a moment and think about what it's like to be ill. What thoughts does it generate? Does it feel restrictive and confining? When you don't feel good, does your world shrink to the point that you only see your life through the condition of your physical body? Does that make you frustrated or angry? Do you find that being sick serves a purpose because it gives you the permission to slow down from the hectic pace of your life? Does it elicit the nurturing and attention you crave?

Are you the kind of person who'll get yourself out of bed even when you feel weak and your muscles ache so much that it would be easier to fall back into bed and pull the covers over your head? Do you identify with your illness by using phrases such as: "I have cancer," "my cholesterol problem," or "I have heart disease"? Do you see your condition as meaningful—trying to tell you that something isn't working? Do you think it's a wake-up call, alerting you that something needs to change?

How you answer these questions reveals the kind of relationship you might develop with an illness, should one occur, and they disclose your perception. Your responses offer insight into the treatments you'll gravitate toward and the role you'll play in the healing process. Most important, they reveal where you'll need to start: with your thoughts. They're behind your emotions and are responsible for your attitudes and beliefs, determining your viewpoint. Thoughts are your inner navigator and serve as the attractants of your experience. They alone determine the quality and substance of your health.

CHAPTER 6

Thoughts as an Inner Navigator

If we're to truly uncover why we become ill, we must begin by understanding what thoughts are, how they work, and why they have so much influence on every aspect of our being—mental, emotional, physical, and soulful. However, trying to do so poses an interesting paradox. Do we try to understand them psychologically or scientifically?

Psychologically, we know that thoughts:

- Exist on some level because we can see their influence on our behavior

- Drive what we say and act upon

- Serve as the attractants of our experiences—so what we think, we become

- Establish the emotional charges we attach to them

- Build on themselves repetitively and form our memories and beliefs

- Are the source of our perceptions, stories, habits, and comfort zones

- Determine how we interact with the outer world—and how it affects us internally

- Influence our relationships and how we interact with others

- Are perceived by the brain as real (although intrinsically, they aren't), thus influencing our perception of reality

Yet scientifically, we know very little about the subject because there are no experiments or blind studies that can produce consistent evidence that thoughts even exist, let alone provide answers to many of the questions we have about them. Among other things, we wonder: *What is the nature of a thought? Is there a spiritual impetus behind what we think? Do thoughts have an energy component that somehow acts as an invisible attractor? Why is it that they can't be described compactly and precisely by anyone other than their creator? If they're merely electrochemical stimuli, how do they trigger a series of observations that are formed into something that has meaning and substance? What determines the emotional charge that should be attached to a thought? Is it the memory of our experiences or is it the soul's way of moving us into action? And of course, why are we the product of our prevailing habitual thoughts?*

Actually, that last question can be scientifically answered because through the efforts to try to understand why we create habitual thoughts, we've gained a better understanding of how the brain works. Scientifically, we've learned that it's an open system, meaning that it's constantly receiving and exchanging information both externally and internally. This give-and-take can be seen as electrochemical impulses moving from one hemisphere to the other and from one lobe to another. When a person engages in similar types of thinking, the neural structure of the brain reorganizes itself so that it can more effectively recognize and accommodate those consistent patterns. Even though the brain is capable of handling many different kinds of external and internal stimuli, it tends to become resistant to accepting new input when mental patterns are repeated, thus limiting the kinds of thoughts produced and the scope of a person's ideas.

We've learned that the brain is no different than any other part of the body. It, too, seeks to survive and thrive and recognizes that it can't do so if it's limited by repetition. Consequently, when it finds itself in a potentially destructive thought pattern, it will reorder its functions by creating new neural pathways, making it possible to reorganize into a higher, more complex level of operation. It's this higher state that increases the communication between parts of the brain that weren't previously interacting. Most important, we know that the brain doesn't just change once in a while; it's an ongoing process.

When the brain repatterns itself, remarkable alterations take place. It becomes more open and receptive to the creation of new thought and mental clarity increases. Information that appeared to be unrelated and deemed unusable— meaning it didn't fit into the repetitive patterns of thinking—is now somehow connected, and as a result, new choices become available. The capacity to learn increases as does the use of intuition. Creativity is activated, and we find ourselves wanting to try new things and to move beyond what's familiar. We're better equipped to cope with challenges because we're more mentally and emotionally stable. We engage in life more positively and interact with people more confidently. Perceptions shift, and we find ourselves not repeating the same patterns of thinking or telling the same old stories. We experience better health because we're creating more supportive thoughts.

While it's impossible to prove at this time, there are a few scientists who believe that the force behind this reorganization and repatterning is more than the brain's need to survive. They believe that it's somehow connected to the soul's need to restore health to the physical, and the only way to do so is to repair the mental state.

The Nature of Thought

A thought is nothing more than a metaphor—one that has meaning and substance to its creator, while at the same time providing an association so that the brain can do something with the information it offers. The brain relies solely on associations to make the connections needed for it to gain understanding, so if the thought doesn't make sense or can't metaphorically provide the right link, the brain will add the necessary details by connecting it with a past experience. In doing so, it triggers a myriad of similar thoughts that will help it determine what to do with the data and how to act on it. By connecting with something familiar, we're able to gain clarity and find meaning in our experiences. However, when the brain isn't able to quickly match an idea with something we know, then its tendency is to deem the concept unusable and dismiss it.

Thoughts serve as the foundation of our existence because they mark our life's events. They connect us with the past, bring us into the present, and offer direction for the future. Yet contrary to what we've been conditioned to believe, they aren't our masters, meaning that they don't control us. Free will is our very nature, and we can change our thoughts anytime we choose to—that is, of course, if we're willing to move beyond what's tried and true.

The purpose of thought is to reveal where we are mentally, emotionally, physically, and spiritually at the precise moment the idea was created, and to reveal if the metaphor it's offering is of any value. If we decide that it does have merit, then we exercise free will by accepting its information and acting on it. On the other hand, if we conclude it's just a duplication of other thoughts supporting a perception, habit, or comfort zone, then we choose to create a new idea.

Thoughts intend to create a more expanded sense of reality by shifting our focus from external to internal, as our human nature is to always see the obvious and look outside of ourselves for answers. By going inward, we're able to get in touch with how outside events are affecting us on the inside. We're able to experience the emotional charges we're adding to our thoughts and use our bodies to tell us if what we're thinking is worth hanging on to and repeating in the future. Perhaps it needs to be changed because of the emotional distress and physical stress it's creating.

Thoughts act as our inner navigators, offering direction and guidance. Through their metaphors, they tell us where we are, where we're going, and what we need to do in order to reach our intended destinations. They make sense of our experiences and help us figure things out. Our thoughts provide insight, propose alternative solutions, create new ideas, help in decision making, and generate emotions so we can determine what to do with them. Thoughts reveal what we want, need, and desire. They'll tell us when the ideas we're creating aren't really ours, but a reflection of someone else's mind—and they'll even tell us when we're thinking too much.

We define who we are by the quality of our thoughts, and we express that through our behavior. If they foster self-confidence, then we act accordingly. On the other hand, if they portray the image of a victim, then we'll play that role, too, and blame others for our misfortunes. If our thoughts are unhealthy, then we engage in detrimental activities and have a harmful lifestyle.

Through the quality of what we think, we're able to see where we're placing our mental energies. If they're focused externally, we'll find ourselves looking to others for approval and acceptance, responding as mental robots rather than thinking for ourselves. If we're looking within, we'll take on the role of an observer and exercise free will to liberate ourselves from others' thinking. In doing so, we'll stop compromising who we really are and allow ourselves to bring forth our natural gifts.

The Anatomy of Thought

Thoughts are the lifeline between our inner and outer worlds. They serve as the weavers of what we learn and the wisdom we hold inside. By interlacing these two realms, we're able to function in an expanded reality and view our experiences in a more holistic way. The ability to create thoughts is limitless. The only boundaries are self-imposed as a result of what we've learned. While what we think creates different behavior and attracts varied experiences, its makeup is consistent. Thoughts consist of awareness, data, emotions, memories, associations, connections, polarity, and change.

Awareness

All thought is triggered by some state of awareness, no matter whether it's what we observe through our five physical senses or what we feel as a result of our inner knowing, our intuition. Awareness is the catalyst for thinking and lets the brain determine which thoughts should be created. We're able to match them with our observations, and thus make sense of them. Awareness heightens our sensitivity both mentally and emotionally and tells the brain which thoughts to multiply, which ones to eliminate, and which ones to act on. It directs the focus of mental activities and determines the emotional charge that should be attached to each thought. It alerts the brain to impending danger and signals when all is well. Awareness makes it possible for us to observe the obvious while at the same time uncovering the hidden meanings behind our experiences. It activates the search for and recovery of information stored in our short- and long-term memory.

Data

All thought is rich with data that makes it possible for the brain to make its associations and connections. When a thought is first created, it's void of any emotional charge, so there's tremendous clarity in the information it offers. We experience this as an epiphany, a moment of realization, a flash of insight, or the proverbial lightbulb going off in our heads; and we know deep inside that the information it offers is accurate. These ideas are associated with inner wisdom and are initiated by our intuition. Consequently, we rely on our instincts to direct us in how we should act them out.

If, for whatever reason, we don't immediately act on our impulses, the brain will begin the association process and the quality of the data being offered will change dramatically. At this point, the material will be matched with a past experience, and it will change from wisdom to a memory. As such, the information will be labeled and an emotional charge will be attached to it, which will tell the brain whether it's usable or should be dismissed. Anytime data is tagged like this, it's altered in a way that eliminates its clarity and diminishes the opportunity for change. The brain would rather deal with familiar data than try to figure out what to do with something that has no precedent.

Emotions

The labeling of a thought occurs the second an emotional charge is added to it—positive or negative, it makes no difference. By doing this, the brain knows how it should process the information and how the data is affecting us internally. Emotions mastermind every aspect of our being. Mentally, they determine the quality of the thoughts, direct the brain in its association process, and help it make the necessary connections to move forward. Physically, they inform the brain of what's happening beneath the surface of our skin. They influence the voluntary bodily processes such as muscle coordination, and the involuntary ones such as the release of hormones in the fight-or-flight response, bladder and bowel control, breathing, and heart rate. Energetically, they change the flow in the body and bring attention to where the physical self is being affected emotionally. They impact the mind/body communication network and reveal when we're energetically exhausted or energetically vitalized.

Memories

Memories are repetitive thoughts that become fixed in our behavior. They're what we remember and what the brain relies upon to make the associations needed in order to act on incoming data. A memory is created whenever the brain labels repetitive thoughts that are charged with similar emotional reactions.

Each individual memory is a microcosm of our life that has become preserved in time. They're the fodder for our stories and responsible for the formation of habits, comfort zones, and perceptions. The problem with them—and the reason they seem to have such a strong grip on our thinking—is because the brain, in its need to make an association, will seek out only the memories that have the strongest emotional charge attached to them. This means that any incoming data that's vaguely similar in its content and feel will be automatically attached to a compatible memory even if the data really isn't well matched. It's this constant, ongoing need to make an association that distorts things to the point that it's difficult to recall the original experience.

Associations

Associations are a necessary part of the thought process because they tell the brain what the next step should be and when to act on the data it's receiving. Without them, the brain would become immobilized with an overabundance of data and be unable to function. As the receiver of data, it must categorize, compartmentalize, and match everything with a recent experience or a long-term memory. It accomplishes this task by associating new information with existing material that isn't part of the actual experience. These links are made through emotional labeling, and there's no intellectual reasoning or logic tied to the event.

When an experience is matched with a memory, we're able to remember it, find meaning in it, act on it, and explain the behavior associated with it. It's helpful if we see associations as the autopilot of the brain, for they orchestrate this process without our having to think about it. Whenever there's a connection, the associative mind files those experiences together in the same organizing memory for future use.

Connections

Connections occur once the preceding process is completed and the brain remembers how to act on the experience. Unlike associations that match events with labeled memories, connections link them with behaviors. This is how we're able to understand events and use them to make decisions. Connections expand the memory by adding time, space, and activity to it. They re-create it mentally and physically and bring it to the forefront of our thinking. In doing so, they bring the recollection to life rather than leaving it stored in our mental archives. This process helps us step back from emotional charges and de-energize them so that we're able to recall the original experience. Connections make it possible for us to cease thinking about doing something; instead, we just do it.

Polarity

Thoughts are polarized: Their underlying creation is activated by either attention or intention. The former is the mental activity of focusing. This helps the brain look for certain features and cues that will lead it to the data it needs and tell it what to do. Attention relies on the physical senses for gathering information and has an external focus. In the perceptional process, the brain needs a place to start—a point of departure for getting data—and requires something to ensure that it will stay focused on the task at hand. The "something" is attention, which lets it observe and examine the overall situation so that it gets the data necessary to begin the association process.

For example, attention uses awareness to look for specific similar qualities of experiences and objects. Once those are identified, attention assigns them a function and relationship with other experiences and objects. This forms the basic framework the mind needs to make its associations and draw on history. The phenomenon of attention has such an all-encompassing effect on the brain's perceptual processes that we're seldom aware of its activity until we recognize a repetitive pattern of thought, experience, or behavior.

Intention, on the other hand, is an emotional activity we use to identify why we want to gather the information we do. It's focused on searching for the meaning behind our thoughts and experiences. This filter eliminates everything that doesn't match with what we want to find, while at the same time helping us concentrate on getting what we desire. Although the brain can search rapidly through a great deal of data acquired through attention, intention focuses on the data that will give us what we need in order to take action.

Paying attention is much easier to do if we know what we want to focus on, and it's the perceptional process of intention that tells the brain what to look for and why. It's what edits out all other data that could act as a distraction. It also compensates for our mental blind spots and uses associations as a backdrop for figuring out what we need to do. Unlike attention, where we're seldom aware of its activities, we're very conscious of intention because we make a deliberate decision to search for something, and we use emotions to tell us if we've found it or not.

Change

Norman Vincent Peale said, "Change your thoughts and you change your world." How true this statement is because every thought created offers the opportunity to change the one that preceded it. When you shift your perception and see this catalyst for change, then you liberate your thinking from the mental limitations created by your conditioning. You find yourself seeing your outer world differently. You become more engaged in life and are more open to trying new things, and how you interact with others shifts significantly. Altering thoughts is a skill that can be developed just like any other. It begins with consciously deciding to take action and identifying the thoughts you want to work on.

Once the process gets going, pay close attention to the occasions where you changed your mind and consciously review them. This allows you to monitor the quality of your thoughts and reevaluate the associations you're making. You'll uncover whether your brain has accepted the new data and is creating fresh associations or whether it's still trying to maintain old ones. It's also helpful to verbalize that you've changed your mind about something, as this will minimize self-doubt and help build your confidence in your ability to create new thoughts.

Thoughts and the Law of Attraction

Thoughts are merely vibration, and when radiating from the body energetically they serve as the attractants of our experiences. This means that what we think, we attract, and vice versa. The moment a thought is created and labeled with an emotion it takes on a life of its own and leaves the body as an energetic message, transmitting its intention to find anyone who can help it in the realization of its purpose. Like Morse code, it's repeatedly broadcasting: *Is there anyone out there who has shared a similar thought and emotional charge? Is there anyone who can provide the necessary data for an association to be made?*

When that thought finds a recipient, there's an unspoken energetic dance and intermingling of ideas that takes place. The thoughts of the sender and the receiver connect, and data transfers. In this connection, the recipient's thought is altered and more thoughts are created. After the exchange is completed, the original thought, like a boomerang, returns to its sender in the form of awareness, and the brain begins its association and connection process. This explains why we tend to attract the same experiences and people over and over again.

This energetic exchange is much like the communication process we engage in physically. If we find someone who is like us and has similar thoughts, our interaction is productive—both people get what they need. However, unlike conversations with people who are different from us and who create tension and stress, the vibrational process will only engage when there's a match. It's important to note that this takes place whether thoughts are spoken or not and that the quality of the data we receive is in direct proportion to what we send out. In other words, thoughts created out of confusion attract the same and those that are clear and concise receive replies in kind.

If the intention behind the message is to support feeling bad about ourselves, then we'll attract people and experiences who will do just that. On the other hand, if we're sick and tired of being down and change our thoughts and the emotional charges attached to them, then we'll attract those that will mirror our new concepts in words and behaviors. This means that the ability to transform, improve, and heal ourselves and control our environment isn't a theory—it's a reality.

How Fast a Thought Travels

The speed of a thought is dependent on the emotional charge attached to it. The stronger the negative energy, the faster it goes, and the more positive it is, the slower it travels. While this may not be what we'd like to hear, there's a reason for this anomaly: conditioning. Let's face it, we're not trained to march to our own drummers or encouraged to express how we feel. We're not raised to believe that we can heal ourselves or be the masters of our own destiny.

We're conditioned to be behaviorally compliant so that other people will accept us, like us, and even love us. We're disciplined to fit into our familial and social structures; and we're chastised, rejected, and ostracized when we try to think out of the box or act differently. We're encouraged to look and act like everyone else. As a result of the personal compromise we feel any time we find ourselves having to act against our inner natures, we attach negative emotional charges to doing so and continue to reinforce those vibrations over and over again until they become the pervasive patterns of thinking and behavior.

The outcome is that our brain, over the course of time, will rework itself to primarily accept only thoughts that support conditioning and that are charged with negative emotions. In doing so, we're able to quickly make associations, connect those with a memory, and use them to make a decision (whether a precise match or not). Then we move on to the next idea. It's easier and quicker for such thoughts to find energetically matching recipients because there are so many people who share similar training.

However, let's shift our perception and look at it another way. If our external world's experiences are merely a reflection of what we've acknowledged to be true as the result of conditioning, then perhaps quickly attracting negative experiences is our brain's way of alerting us that the repetitive thought patterns are potentially detrimental to its well-being and to our overall health. Maybe the sheer momentum of recurrence is encouraging us to change.

With this new outlook in mind, it could be that experiences charged with positive emotions move slower so that we can recognize what we need to shift or how we've changed. Perhaps the decreased speed allows us to take the mental pause needed to reevaluate the quality of our thoughts. Thus we won't blindly attract what we don't want. The lesser velocity may enable us to make the necessary course corrections along the way rather than waiting until we hit that proverbial brick wall—and lie there wondering what just happened. Maybe by going slower, we can see how our thoughts are affecting our body and then harness positive ideas to improve the quality of our health.

Thoughts and the Health of the Body

Is there a connection between what we think and what happens in our body? Absolutely, and science is finally beginning to catch up with what the ancient metaphysicians believed for thousands of years: *What we think and how we feel are revealed in the body.* We now know that our nervous, immune, and endocrine systems are in constant communication, not only with each other, but also with our thoughts. The chemical messages tied to them give instructions. What this means is that every thought is affecting the body to some degree, whether it's linked to an "up" or "down" emotion. However, we're finding that we have to look out for the negatively charged thoughts because they have the strongest chemical messages and create the greatest chaos in the body. They have the biggest impact on the immune system, and over the course of time are responsible for the most wear and tear on its ability to ward off infections, bacteria, and viruses that will ultimately present themselves as illness.

Candace Pert, Ph.D., author of *Molecules of Emotion,* tells us that physical and emotional stress actually change the body's ability to function properly. She reveals that negative thoughts and emotional stress can produce a chemical imbalance that expresses itself in the form of despair and hopelessness, which triggers the suppression of the immune system. Her research shows that since everything is energy, we can conclude that there's no difference between a thought's energy and that of the body; and it doesn't seem to make a difference whether the idea is being triggered externally or internally. If it's charged with a negative emotion, it directly suppresses the immune system and can make us sick. It can even kill us.

There are basically two kinds of thoughts: healthy and unhealthy. If we want to see how the latter increases our susceptibility to illness, we don't have to look any further than the common cold. For centuries, it has been widely believed that emotions such as grief and disappointment make us more prone to minor respiratory infections such as colds and flu. This has now been confirmed scientifically. In one study, subjects were asked to track the number of hassles they experienced on a daily basis and then write down how those events made them feel mentally, emotionally, and physically. The results showed that the individuals who seemed to take things in stride had fewer health ramifications. On the other hand, the people who described feeling beaten down, worn out, and tired of all the stressors had more respiratory infections. The research even showed that typically a few days before the onset of the respiratory infection there would be a rise in the number of irritating events and a corresponding decrease in the ability to deal with them. The conclusion was that the repetition of stressful thoughts associated with the hassles and the anxiety wore down the immune system, thus increasing susceptibility to the common cold.

This happened when the subjects' thoughts transmuted to a belief that life is just one continual hassle after another. Not only did they have a distorted belief, they had a soured attitude toward life because they view it as a perpetual disappointment. As a medical intuitive, I see the common cold and flu as the outcome of thoughts becoming acidic (sour) and as a result changing the pH in both the digestive and immune systems. This creates a chemical imbalance that produces the ideal environment for the virus responsible for these illnesses. Grief and sadness are acidic emotions and energetically reside in the lungs—grief in the right and sadness in the left.

Every ache and pain sends a message to the brain that something we're thinking and feeling is creating a physical problem. Our body is asking for help, requesting that we immediately change what's causing the trouble. While it may sound somewhat odd to say, and can definitely be hard to believe, pain is the brain's kindest benefactor. It not only tells what thoughts and emotions are at fault, it reveals where in the body we're holding onto them. If we take the time to listen, it will even tell us what we need to do to change. Now comes the caveat: Usually, we need to alter a belief. This isn't an easy task, because conditioning has taught us to hold tightly to our beliefs. They represent the thoughts we accept as being true.

When Thoughts Become Beliefs

Beliefs are formed when thoughts become fixed in both memory and behavior. If we were to remove the *be* and the *f* from the word *belief,* we'd find the word *lie,* which is exactly what a group of thoughts turn into once they become carefully archived as a memory and stored in the brain as a truth. Beliefs are specialized thoughts charged with observations and expectations that have grown inflexible over the course of time. They cause us to get set in our ways, thus becoming the source of our comfort zones and habits.

Because of their rigidity, the brain deems beliefs factual and real—but they aren't. They're illusory. Yet they still have such a hold that we allow them to create the mental limitations that restrict our thinking. They're really just used to focus on a specific behavior—something our conditioning invented to help us remember how we should think and act. They're like magicians, creatively leading us to believe something untrue. They tell the brain to pull rabbits from a hat, even though the hat isn't real.

Before thoughts are transmuted into beliefs, they serve an important purpose. To begin with, they provide data with the consistent emotional charges that the brain needs to make associations and connect the dots. They help the brain categorize experiences and discern meaning. They reflect the data we learned from specific situations and recall it if we experience the same situation in the future. They ensure only the safest and most predictable and reliable information comes through so that the right connections can be made—connections that ensure our survival and offer the greatest opportunity for our wishes to be realized. However, once those thoughts are transmuted into beliefs, they become the perceived masters of our thinking. Therein lies the problem.

Letting go of our beliefs isn't an easy feat because the brain has grown accustomed to relying on them. Consequently, it's going to hang on to them like a prized possession. It's like we're on autopilot, engaging in life by rote rather than being consciously responsible for what we're thinking, saying, or doing. We act as though we aren't even aware of our beliefs or have forgotten them.

When we do decide to change, our challenge begins with sorting through those on file, and then calling up the right one. Once we find it, then we have to commit the mental and emotional time to evaluate it, explore it, and recognize the behavior associated with it. Then we're ready to act.

However, since transformation isn't easy or comfortable, and because we have an unspoken identity attached to our beliefs, the task becomes more daunting emotionally. Our beliefs help us look like everyone else and allow us to fit in. They create the false personifications that influence how other people see us and interact with us. They discourage thinking and create a mental laziness that supports sticking with what's tried-and-true, and they encourage taking the path of least resistance. In doing so, we remain behaviorally predictable and malleable, both of which discourage change and the creation of different thoughts.

How do we uncover the beliefs responsible for creating the mental limitations we struggle with everyday—the same ones that cause us to feel compromised and lead us to believe we're somehow flawed or inadequate, or worse yet, unlovable? We use our emotions. We look at our fears, because they create unpleasant thoughts and have the strongest reactions tied to them. It's through them that we uncover the expectations associated with our beliefs and discover just how much of ourselves we've compromised. And while beliefs aren't real—emotions are.

CHAPTER 7

Emotions:
Our Internal Barometer

The next step in the process of understanding why we become ill is learning more about emotions and the important role they play in affecting immunity. They're strong mental or instinctive reactions to a thought or an event. They may be psychic or physical reactions that are subjectively experienced as strong knowing or physiologically involving changes that prepare the body for immediate vigorous action, an agitation of the passions, or any strong reaction such as joy, sorrow, hate, or anger.

Emotions are aroused energy intended to get our attention, and their purpose is to move us into action. They're attached to our thoughts, so the brain can quickly and effectively make its associations and connections to our memories and beliefs. They're what give strength, persistence, and predictability to our thoughts. They help us make sense of why we do the things we do. Emotions oversee what we think, constantly monitoring and regulating it so that we don't find ourselves engaging in self-sabotaging cogitation or destructive behavior. They tell us when our thoughts are betraying us and causing us to compromise who we are; and conversely, they let us know when thoughts are supporting who we are and attracting experiences that add to the quality of our lives.

The root word of emotion is *emote*, meaning to give expression to, which is what we're suppose to do when we experience these sensations. We're to use our emotions to express how we feel about something, and they let other people know when they've overstepped our boundaries by alerting them to the fact they've hurt our feelings. We aren't supposed to suppress our emotions or hide them as our conditioning encourages. Neither should we bury them deep inside, allowing them to fester and build on themselves until we have an emotional meltdown—or worse yet, a physical breakdown. Discouraging expression is sadly shortsighted because there are times in life when logic isn't enough or when it can't tell us what to do, such as guiding us through predicaments that require us to act quickly and instinctively. In these kinds of situations, the value of our emotions is unquestionable because they instantaneously offer a call to action and they instantly point us in a direction that has worked well in the past. When push comes to shove, it's emotions that save our life, not logic.

Feelings and Emotions Aren't the Same

Although the words *feelings* and *emotions* are used synonymously, they're not the same either in meaning or in how they affect the physical body.

Feelings

Feelings are merely thoughts without an emotional label attached to them. They're just information, pure and simple. When we share them, we're giving unbiased information that we don't have an attachment to, meaning we aren't trying to convince people of anything. We aren't using anger or guilt to manipulate them to act because we believe it's in their best interest (even if it isn't). They're only an expression of what we've learned, what we've experienced, what we know instinctively, and they reflect our opinions.

Feelings, like a compass, tell us where we are. They don't relate whether it's good or bad, and they don't let us know how we should proceed forward. They supply the brain with the information it needs to understand situations and at the same time identify if there are any problems created as a result. Feelings are a catalyst in helping the brain sort through the barrage of data it receives so that it can discern what's viable and reliable. They act as impartial receptors for data gathered through the physical senses and then cross-check that data against our intuition. In this way, we're able to get a holistic perspective of what's happening in both our outer and inner worlds.

Since feelings are void of emotional charges and the expectations associated with emotions, they don't have any deep psychological implications attached to them. They don't have the need to support old patterns of thinking or perpetuate beliefs. All they do is form mental images and provide insight into how we're sensing and perceiving our experiences. They provide a glimpse into the contents of our psychological coffers: our thoughts, emotions, attitudes, perceptions, stories, and beliefs. And because they aren't a part of its contents, they don't affect the chemical balance of the body, nor do they contribute to the formation of illness.

Emotions

Emotions, on the other hand, are thoughts with a judgment attached to them. By adding an assessment, what we think becomes emotionally charged. This makes it easier for the brain to discern good thoughts from bad and determine what behavior is acceptable. Emotions serve as our internal barometer and are the vehicle our soul uses to help us discern the quality of our ideas. They effectively reveal how what we're experiencing externally is affecting us internally, letting us know when change is necessary and helping us recognize when we're in control or someone else is. They set off an instantaneous chemical chain reaction that alerts us that something is happening that needs our attention. We experience that chemistry change in the form of fight-or-flight responses and stress.

Psychologically, emotions are designed to help the brain in its decision-making process. If negative emotions are attached to thoughts, we'll be sure to stick with decisions that are familiar and that will keep us safe. We'll avoid any choices that have the potential for conflict so we won't have to re-experience the suffering and discomfort they produce. The thoughts with the worst charges tend to get the most attention because of the distractions they create. We try to avoid having to deal with them. Consequently, rather than changing whatever is needed, it's human nature to sweep them under the rug and pretend they don't exist.

However, suppressing unpleasant emotions isn't good for the body or the mind, because when we do so, we put ourselves into a fight-or-flight state and set off a chemical chain reaction that inhibits the body from functioning properly. Whenever this situation occurs, we become flooded with an abundance of hormones, which makes it more difficult to recover and requires more time to correct the imbalance. Mentally, keeping unpleasant emotions hidden inhibits the brain's ability to make associations and connections, causing us to be unable to think clearly. At the same time, it makes negative emotions build quickly on themselves until we find ourselves worrying, fretting, and getting angry.

Whenever this occurs, we find ourselves being held hostage by old beliefs. We complain of being sick and tired of the same old emotional roller coaster, and we make commitments we can't keep, such as vowing to never get into any situation or relationship that will bring these negative emotions to the surface again. An example of the impact such scenarios have on our thinking can be found when someone offers an idea that could solve an ongoing problem we've been complaining about. Rather than being receptive and open, our old emotional patterns immediately negate and dismiss the concept as not being feasible or realistic, and we become distracted by thinking of all of the ways it wouldn't work. The result is that we continue to deal with the issue, repeat the same old behavior, and find ourselves limited by our negative beliefs.

On the other hand, if we were to add a positive emotional charge to a thought, we'd find ourselves eager to expand the thought and flesh it out so we could take action on it. This would play out mentally in decreased activity in the part of the brain that creates negative emotions. The slowdown would quell those worrisome and agitated thoughts, so the brain would be open to new ideas and ready to take on new challenges. Our enthusiasm would rise, as would our excitement. Physically, this energy would only create minuscule physiological changes in our chemistry, thus allowing our bodies to recover more quickly from the biological arousal we were experiencing. We would find ourselves feeling energized, revitalized, and ready to do whatever was needed to get us where we wanted to go. By adding positive emotional charges to our thoughts, we have a much better chance of manifesting what we desire.

Emotions are the first instinctual language we use as children to express our needs, wants, and desires. We learn how to interact with others and find out what behavior is acceptable. We also find out how to manipulate people into seeing that our needs are met. Emotions are used as a means of getting attention, having ourselves heard, and expressing what we're feeling inside. Most of the emotional language we speak mirrors what we've seen, learned, or experienced as children and reflects the influence that other people have had on us.

When our reactions get the kind of response we're seeking, we emotionally and energetically imprint them both in the memory banks of the mind and in the cells of the body. Later in life, when a situation arises that requires a specific kind of response, we go to those archives and draw on them to tell us how to act and react.

Where Do Emotions Come From?

There are actually three different answers to this question—the mind, body, or soul—depending on who we're asking.

They Come from the Mind

If we were asking neuroscientists, they'd tell us that emotions originate in the brain and that there are specific parts of that organ responsible for fear and negative emotions (the amygdala), and sections for love and positive emotions (the nucleus accumbens). They'd say that the seat of emotions lies within the workings of the limbic or emotional brain and involves the biochemical interplay between the thalamus, amygdala, nucleus accumbens, and hippocampus. They'd explain that emotions are triggered by external input from the physical senses—primarily from the senses of sight and hearing—and that it's these signals sent to the thalamus that set off the emotional chain of events.

When the thalamus receives its external data, it moves into action—analyzing, assessing, and translating that data into chemical messages so that the brain can enable us to determine the appropriate action. At this time in the process, we're dealing with feelings, meaning it's still unbiased information. If upon evaluation, the thalamus deems the content a potential risk to our well-being, it sends the message to the amygdala for immediate action. On the other hand, if it decides that an emotional reaction isn't necessary, it sends the message to the neocortex (the thinking part of the brain) for additional analysis.

The amygdala is the seat of fear and negative emotions. Its purpose is to act as an emotional sentinel, responding or reacting to the information it receives. There are two amygdalas in the human brain, one on each side of the organ, and these two almond sized clusters hold the responsibility of seeing that we survive. So when they receive any hint from the thalamus that something can potentially threaten that survival, they send out an instantaneous chemical message that there's a problem. That's what kicks the adrenals into action. They secrete the hormones that alert the entire body to be prepared. At the same time that the message is being sent to the adrenals, the amygdala is also alerting the entire brain, as well as checking in with the hippocampus to see if there's any other pertinent information it needs to be aware of.

The hippocampus is considered the gateway to memory and is the bridge between thought and recollection. It's where we store our beliefs, perceptions, and stories. However, the information held here is different from that in the amygdala. The hippocampus remembers facts and provides the details associated with past experiences, whereas the amygdala deals with the emotional perceptions that go with the facts. The primary function of the hippocampus is to serve the amygdala by registering and making sense of the emotional perceptions it receives, and then connecting those perceptions with past behavior.

Neuroscientist Joseph LeDoux of the Center for Neural Science at New York University described the interplay between the hippocampus and the amygdala very eloquently when he said, "The hippocampus is crucial in recognizing a face as that of your cousin. But it is the amygdala that adds, you don't really like her."

However, another interplay that affects us emotionally is between the hippocampus and the nucleus accumbens, the pleasure part of the brain. Think for a moment of something that makes you happy: the touch of someone you love, the smell of freshly baked bread, hearing children's laughter, or having a puppy lick your face. While all of these create some physiological response, they're nothing like those created by the amygdala. This is because the memories pulled up by the hippocampus around these experiences haven't become distorted with negative emotions, nor are they hidden within false beliefs. They aren't charged with compromise; they're vibrating with love. Consequently, we can remember them as we originally experienced them and recall them as if they just happened yesterday.

They Come from the Body

If we were asking anatomists where emotions come from, we'd hear that they're visceral, because we experience them first in the gut and then in the muscles. They'd explain that it's the bodily sensations we get from what we perceive that send the emotional messages to the brain for interpretation, association, and then connection to a memory. They believe physical and mental functioning are intricately intertwined by a network of nerve bundles that are bidirectional; each is able to affect and alter the other's emotional reaction or response.

To help us better understand the dance between the two, anatomists would refer us to the muscles, which are responsible for movement, the intention behind emotions. The muscles accomplish this motion through a series of sensory impulses that travel the nerve trunks running through them. If we were to trace the pathway of these nerve trunks, we'd find that they attach to a column of tissue called the spinal cord. Then following the spinal cord up to the base of the skull, we'd see that it enters into the brain through a small hole. Anatomists believe it's this attachment of nerves to the various parts of the brain that instructs that organ in how to move forward with the information offered through bodily sensations.

Anatomists would also remind us that all muscles and organs—including the heart and the liver—have these nerve trunks, so they all play an integral part in the information sent to the brain via the spinal cord.

It seems that the muscles and organs also have the capacity to trigger memories of our emotional reactions to specific events. Consequently, if we find ourselves experiencing something that's similar and has a familiar emotional charge to it, we'll sense it in specific parts of the body. For example, we might experience right shoulder tension every time we find ourselves feeling responsible for carrying the weight of the world on our shoulders, or we might have jaw discomfort every time we're in a verbally contentious situation.

The body knows and tells us through the muscles. They'll freeze up, contract, and spasm as if alerting the brain that something is up. And while anatomists can't prove these sensory impulses to the brain via the nerves are actually emotions, they can show that what they evoke is the source of how we experience emotions. To support their findings, they use the examples of how strong negative emotions are gut-wrenching, how they can freeze us in our tracks if we're about to put ourselves in harm's way, how anger changes the functioning of the heart, and how love makes the knees weak and the palms sweaty.

They Come from the Soul

If we were to ask metaphysicians where emotions come from, they'd say, "The soul." They'd remind us that the soul is the core essence of who we are and that its presence can be found energetically in every part of our being: our brain, muscles, organs, glands, and trillions of other cells that make up the physical body. The metaphysicians would reiterate what quantum physicists have believed all along: Everything is energy first and matter second. They'd ask us to remember that the activities of the soul animate the physical body and make it possible for us to discern if we're conducting our lives in or out of alignment with who we truly are.

They'd explain how emotions are the internal barometer the soul uses to alert us when we're engaging in unhealthy thoughts and attracting experiences that aren't in our best interest. They'd prompt us to remember how emotions are used: The stronger the negative emotion, the more we'll feel compromised, therefore creating a greater urgency for change. The stronger the positive emotion, the greater the validation of the fact that thoughts and lifestyle are in alignment with our soul's intentions and desires.

To make their point and help us remember this instant feedback system, they'd ask us to think back to a situation that made us unhappy or caused us to feel energetically drained and emotionally depressed. Were we doing something we wanted to do or fulfilling an obligation? Were we trying to please other people because we didn't want to create conflict or hurt their feelings? Did we feel mentally stuck and trapped? Then they'd ask us to think of something that made us happy—that we loved doing, were excited about, and felt passionate about. Didn't we feel good about ourselves, exude self-confidence, and feel energized? Wasn't our mind eager to try something new?

Since we are energetic in nature, metaphysicians believe that emotions are felt simultaneously throughout the body. They'd support their beliefs by describing the emotional reaction or response as more like a bioenergetic dance of the soul, mind, and body that isn't just bidirectional; it's multidirectional. This means that every part of our body would experience emotions the exact same way and at the same time. The only difference would be in how each expresses emotions. The mind expresses emotions chemically, the body electrically, and the soul energetically.

Metaphysicians would challenge the idea that memories are stored only in the mind, believing that they're also kept in every cell of the body. When the emotional alarm is set off, the cells carrying that emotional memory become active. They'd explain how the process works by linking it to the activities of the *neurohormonal pores.* These are strategically placed at specific sites in the body and lie just beneath the surface of the skin. They're part of the vascular autonomic system and serve as receptors for energy-carrying information that falls beneath the threshold of the five physical senses because it's vibrational in nature.

Within these neurohormonal pores are neurotransmitters that carry the information to the brain and the other parts of the body for interpretation, association, and connection with stored memories. Once the data is received, the body parts react or respond according their own needs. The brain connects the new input with what's been gathered through the five physical senses. The muscles, organs, and glands link it through the electrochemical messages they receive from the brain. The soul associates it vibrationally through the activities of the cells.

It's helpful to remember that we're constantly being bombarded with information, even when we can't detect it with our physical senses. Consequently, we're going to experience emotional reactions and responses to some degree, whether we're consciously aware of what triggered them or not. The metaphysicians connect this phenomenon to the Law of Magnetic Attraction—*What we think, we attract. What we attract, we think.* Each of us is constantly transmitting thoughts even when we've long forgotten them. Those thoughts, because of their vibrational nature, will return to their sender along with the same emotional charge attached to them when they were first transmitted. Rather than being received in a way that allows the brain to be the first to react or respond to them, they'll be taken in through the neurohormonal pores, so the cells, then the body, and finally the brain will react or respond.

As a closing thought on where emotions come from, metaphysicians would remind us of how the mind can be conditioned to avoid dealing with emotions and even taught how to suppress their expression. However, the cells can't do the same, because the soul uses the body as a diagnostic tool, revealing how and where our emotions are affecting us. In doing so, the mind has no choice but to engage in the process of evaluating the quality of our thoughts and dealing with the emotional charges attached to them. The soul uses emotions as a means of giving us a glimpse into what's going on within our flesh.

There Are Just Two Kinds of Emotions

When looking at emotions, there appear to be a multitude of them. However, there are actually only two: *fear* and *love.* Yet within these two we'll find the source of the all of apparent emotions we have and express, and we'll uncover their underlying implications. We'll discover how they're determining our thoughts, manipulating our behavior, impacting the quality of our lives, and controlling our health. Since emotions are defined in terms of how they affect us biologically and psychologically, it's easy to understand why it's so important to get in touch with them, learn how to deal with them, and bring them to expression. In our willingness to do so, we'll learn how to use them constructively to free ourselves from the mental oppression created by our stories, beliefs, and perceptions.

Fear

There are two descriptive definitions of fear. The first is **F**alse **E**xpectations **A**ctually **R**ealized; the second is **F**alse **E**vidence **A**ppearing **R**eal. The key to both of them is that they reveal where fear comes from—conditioning—and that it's externally driven.

We aren't born afraid, even though our brain comes equipped with a fear alarm. Instead, this emotion is a gift we get from interacting with other people. That's not to imply that they mean to cause us harm, because for the most part they're trying to help us become better, to fit into our familial and social structure so that we can be accepted, liked, and loved. They just try to protect us. Yet they unknowingly infect us with their fears, not realizing that emotions are contagious and will multiply like a virus. They don't understand how one person's fears become another's and how those terrors can lie dormant in the brain and body until the right experience causes them to surface. Little do they know how their anxieties mutate when the recipients add their own emotional charges, nor do they comprehend to what extent they impact others' lives or health. If they did, they wouldn't be so quick to share their fears with those they love and care about.

Fear is the source of all negative responses, including: *anger, rage, fury, terror, anxiety, resentment, wrath, exasperation, indignation, animosity, irritability, hatred, denial, grief, apprehension, nervousness, concern, worry, misgiving, dread, fright, betrayal, apathy, intimidation, rejection, criticism, frustration, shame, suffering,* and *sadness.* They're responsible for phobias, panic disorders, post-traumatic stress syndrome, and obsessive-compulsive behavior.

The problem with fear is that it creates a false sense of security and protection that puts up mental limitations, which prevent us from fully engaging in life. Fear puts us on guard and makes us anxious and defensive. It breeds suspicion and doubt and causes us to not trust anyone, ourselves included. It fosters envy, jealously, helplessness, disappointment, despair, and hopelessness. It supports separation and encourages isolation. It's responsible for our knee-jerk reactions and causes us to lash out at others, to be hurtful in our words and actions. Fear creates emotional pain and wounds and is the impetus behind victim behavior.

Love

Love, on the other hand, connects us with our emotions in a positive way so that we can use them as they were intended: to be catalysts for change. The presence of love creates a sense of inner peace, making it possible for us to become a silent observer of our thoughts, emotional expressions, and behavior. Love adds stability and predictability to our life and quells our fears. It provides the emotional strength and courage needed to face what frightens us and to conquer it. It inspires us to seek in life what we desire rather than fostering beliefs that we aren't worthy of what we desire. It views life and all of its experiences the same way the soul does, seeing the opportunity to learn, grow, change, and spiritually evolve.

When we love who we are, we feel physically strong, self-confident, and self-reliant and experience a personal resiliency that allows us to go with the flow of life. Our minds are open and receptive to new ideas, and the thoughts we send out will vibrationally attract our desire for new opportunities and different quality relationships. Mentally, we're better equipped to deal with the challenges life presents us, and as Dale Carnegie said, "We're able to turn lemons into lemonade." The energy of self-love is transformative and empowers us to reach beyond the self-perceived limitations created by our fears. Consequently, it's easier for us to attract what we want rather than what we don't. We're also less inclined to tell our stories and look for the sympathy of others. Love frees our hearts so that we can move through life with an air of grace and self-assurance and be open to receiving affection from others.

Love is the source of all positive emotions, including: *joy, bliss, courage, hope, acceptance, compassion, kindness, devotion, happiness, contentment, delight, gratification, forgiveness, ecstasy, satisfaction, relief, thrill, trust, adoration, pleasure, intimacy, rapture,* and *peace.* It's responsible for an optimistic attitude and good health.

Love and fear can't occupy the same space in the brain or the heart. So at some point in our lives, we're going to have to make a choice as to which one we're going to allow to run our lives. When you look at these two emotions from their health consequences, it becomes a very obvious and straightforward decision.

How Emotions Affect Health

As a medical intuitive, I've sat across from hundreds of people who were dealing with life-threatening illnesses and desired more than anything else to heal themselves. Yet while doing all they thought they should, they weren't getting the results they wanted because they were missing an important piece of the puzzle. They didn't understand that every ache and symptom was the soul's way of using the body to reveal what kinds of emotions were controlling their thinking, lives, and health. They didn't understand that in the land of illness, emotions reign supreme; and they can make us so emotionally fragile and fearful that they can exacerbate the problem rather than heal it. Most important, these individuals didn't understand the health consequences of fear and love.

The Health Consequences of Fear

No one is free of fear, yet some are more fearful than others. This is mostly because of inherent personality traits and how they influence the tolerance we must have to live with this emotion and how we must deal with it. For example: Some personalities are more prone to worrying, which constantly fuels their anxieties. Another type will avoid their worries, pretending they don't exist, yet within their bodies those fears are insidiously spreading and creating new ones. Then there are those who believe they can conquer anything—even their fears—if they just understand them, work hard enough, and struggle and suffer in the process. This personality sees all of these behaviors as the road to freedom and a way to prove to themselves and others that they're really trying, which is a fear in itself. And, finally there are the people who are so frozen by their worries that they allow these emotions to run their lives. They're afraid to go out after dark, that they'll lose their job, that they won't have enough money or time, that something bad is going to happen, they won't be loved, and even that they'll get ill. What this personality doesn't realize is that fear is a self-fulfilling prophecy.

There are six fundamental fears that we all deal with to some degree:

1. Survival
2. The unknown
3. Abandonment
4. Betrayal
5. Rejection
6. Dying

The interesting part about these fears is that they're the root source of the multitude of other doubts we create and experience. For example: the fear of change stems from that of the unknown, worry about financial loss comes from that of survival, dread of being alone has its roots in abandonment issues, concern about becoming ill is related to fear of dying, trust problems are tied up with worry about betrayal, and on and on it goes.

There's yet another interesting part about these six fears: They show up in specific parts of the spine and affect certain nerve trunks of the body and spinal cord. This means that when we experience the six—which we do, have, and will at some point—they're going to affect the health and well-being of our spine and the parts of the body associated with them. We're going to get to live with the chronic back pains and headaches they create until we learn how to free ourselves from their grip.

Physically, fear can also be found in the heart, adrenals, reproductive organs, and spleen. The anxiety that fear creates causes the body to release high levels of cortisol, an agent known to interfere with the functioning of the immune system. As a result, we're more prone to viral and bacterial infections; cancer; autoimmune disorders such as AIDS, lupus, fibromyalgia, chronic fatigue syndrome, and rheumatoid arthritis; asthma; diabetes; digestive problems; degenerative diseases such as multiple sclerosis (MS) and skeletal problems; hypertension; and chronic inflammation in the blood vessel walls and arteries, which increases the potential for heart disease. Psychologically, fear is the source of phobias, addictions, and passive-aggressive and obsessive-compulsive behavior. It's also a contributor to paranoid schizophrenia.

The most important thing to remember about this emotion is that the body can't withstand its effects indefinitely. The mere anticipation of what might happen is enough to trigger the physical affects of fear, and when that happens, the body instantaneously becomes debilitated and experiences stress and emotional suffering. If fear is chronic, it wears down the body's ability to function properly. If sudden, it creates an intense state of the fight-or-flight response that can short circuit and overwhelm the body with a chemical reaction. In many cases, such a situation can result in a heart attack or someone actually dying of fright. The bottom line is that, at some point, we're going to have to address our fears because if we don't they'll take a toll on the body.

The Health Consequences of Love

Love offers us the two things we need the most when dealing with an illness:

1. It prompts the body to secrete oxytocin (the same chemical released during lovemaking), boosting the release of healthy hormones that

support the immune system's effectiveness
and decreasing the stress hormone, cortisol.

2. It provides hope, something we need lots
   of when the fear around illness occupies our
   mind and our body.

Physically, love causes specific electrochemical changes in the body that stimulate the release of endorphins and neuropeptides, which tell the body that all is well. These chemicals have several physical effects: They strengthen the immune system's activities, influence the functioning of individual organs and glands, tell the muscles to relax, and signal the adrenals to calm down. When it comes to healing, love is like taking a heavy dose of ibuprofen. It curbs the flow of pain receptors, which causes the brain to stop fixating on pain. This reprieve allows the mind to focus on something else, like hope.

Psychologically, hope serves as a crucial antidote to fear and has such a powerful influence on the mind and body that people have been known to use it to help heal themselves of supposedly terminal illnesses. Hope is an active emotion, not a passive one like fear. Whereas being afraid immobilizes the brain and creates chemical chaos in the body, hope mobilizes and creates a sense of inner peace. It frees the mind to look for other possibilities, and it unleashes the inner fighter that's so important if we're to heal ourselves. Hope is an action plan, a goal-oriented attitude that requires change, discipline, and most of all, commitment. It isn't "pie in the sky" expectations or wishful thinking, nor can we reap its full benefits if we take a halfhearted, cavalier approach. It requires that we live in its spirit and manage the mind so that it will manifest thoughts that support well-being.

More and more physicians are beginning to realize the importance of hope in the healing process, especially for cancer. An oncologist I work with told me about a patient who was having such severe reactions to the chemotherapy treatments that she was seriously considering stopping them. However, since she was in stage IV breast cancer, he didn't think that would be a good idea. Instead, he suggested they look for other ways to approach the healing process in addition to the drugs.

He did some research and found a new holistic approach that seemed to be showing strong evidence of working well with breast cancer and also helping minimize some of the adverse side effects from chemotherapy. When the woman asked him what the new treatment was, he said, "Hope." That was all she needed to hear, because she hadn't experienced that emotion in some time.

The doctor told me that this patient was on 17 different medications, in addition to the chemotherapy, prior to this new treatment. Then within three months, her cancer was in remission and she was down to only two drugs. When I asked what he thought had changed, he answered, "Hope."

The Next Step in the Healing Process

While understanding how and why emotions affect our health is certainly important if we're to heal ourselves, there's another aspect of emotions we need to take into consideration: the role they play in the development of attitudes, because they form our beliefs, impact our behavior, affect our self-image, color our perception of the outer world, influence how we interact with other people, determine our lifestyle choices, govern how we perceive illness, and control how we treat it.

CHAPTER 8

Never Underestimate
an Attitude

An attitude is more a chronic state of being than anything else. It represents thoughts, opinions, behavioral patterns, emotional reactions, and perceptions that become fixed in the body and fixed memories that either discourage or embrace changes. Attitudes are a self-fulfilling continuum between illness and good health. A positive one promotes well-being, and a negative one ensures poor health.

There are many words for attitudes, such as *outlook, approach, inclination, tendency, demeanor,* and *stance.* However, the two that best describe them are *moods* and *disposition.* The former tell us where we are emotionally, and the latter lets us know where we are mentally. Moods reveal the short-term impact of our attitudes, and disposition shows the long-term. Both offer insight into how we see ourselves and the value we place on what we bring to the world.

Attitudes are associated more with thought patterns that support our emotions than with emotions themselves. They color our perception of the outer world and form the perceptions we have of how we fit into it. The emotional charge associated with them lingers in the mind and body and is difficult to change because attitudes are meant to keep us from having to revisit the same hurtful emotional experiences over and over again. Consequently, they're like pots that are always on the verge of boiling over.

Attitudes serve as the watchdogs for our minds and create the mental buffers needed to help protect them from having to continually endure a barrage of emotions. They're primarily influenced by the reactions we have to external influences and are usually directed toward the tangibles of life: objects, people, situations, experiences, and lifestyles. If our responses were favorable, then the attitudes we created around them would be positive. Conversely, if we experience strong negative reactions to those external factors, then the attitudes we form would amplify that feedback because we'd continue to rehash it.

Attitudes are the by-product of our emotional reactions and reflect the residual impact they've had on us, both mentally and physically. Fundamentally, attitudes are recycled emotions that continue to recirculate until they become so entrained in our thinking and behavior that they eventually dictate how we live our lives and ultimately alter our thinking. Unlike emotions, however, attitudes don't create instantaneous chemical changes in the body. They just see to it that those made by emotional reactions are perpetuated, meaning that they make the chemical shifts chronic. In the case of illness, it's the never-ending recycling of negative replays that eventually wears down the mind and body and drains them of the vital energy they need to function properly. The long-term effects are the creation of distorted beliefs and the materialization of low levels of apprehension and nervousness, which show up in our moods and disposition.

Attitudes are the result of learned behavior. They're the perceptions developed based on past experiences and are the outcome of our conditioning and what we experienced as kids. In fact, the majority of the attitudes we have and get to deal with as adults were formed during childhood. The problem with attitudes is that they magnify our early experiences and exaggerate the emotional charges associated with them until they're distorted into something bigger and more significant than they were when originally experienced. This is when they turn into beliefs.

Let's use the example of a teacher telling a boy that he'll never be good at math because he can't add or subtract. Now that might seem pretty innocuous, until we hear that the teacher delivered the message in a stern, forceful, and loud tone of voice. Then let's add to the experience the element of embarrassment and humiliation that the child felt in front of his schoolmates. To make it even more emotionally charged, let's imagine that the boy didn't want to go home and tell his parents because he felt that they'd be disappointed—or worse yet, would punish him. With all of these factors added to the event and then reinforced every time teachers or, later in life, bosses raise their voices or express disappointment in his abilities, it's easy to see how this person could develop a pessimistic attitude and distorted beliefs about what he's capable of achieving. The really unfortunate aspect of this kind of attitude is that it will limit the person's opportunities for his entire life because he believes it's true.

If we were to step back and look at the difference between how emotions and attitudes affect the body, it would be easier for us to understand why it's the attitudes we have to watch out for. After all, they're what erode the mind and body. In the case of emotions, human physiology is designed to handle and offset the sudden impact of emotions. It has within its anatomy all kinds of cancelling systems such as the immediate release of the "all is well" endorphins in the brain when the fight-or-flight state is triggered. These chemicals produce an instantaneous urge to empty the bladder so that we release the stress toxins; a change in our breathing to rapid and shallow so that we can exhale the stress toxins; and sweating, which is the body's way of releasing stress hormones through the pores of the skin.

However, what the body isn't designed to do is handle or offset the chronic mental stress and emotional distress created by attitudes. It can't use the same innate defense systems that deal with sudden threats to defuse attitudes because those systems don't manage thoughts or the association and connection processes. This means that attitudes are responsible for initiating the breakdown and deterioration of physical health and the weakening of the immune system. They're the source of the onset of illness, not emotions, which are a factor only when they go unchecked and create attitudes that take away the pleasure, joy, and passion in life. Unless we plan to undergo a lobotomy, the single way to rid the body of our attitudes is to change them. When we do so, we not only alter our mental state, we transform physically, too.

The most common attitudes that have a negative impact on our physical health and overall well-being are: *depressed, melancholy, resentful, hostile, frustrated, aggressive, disappointed, irritated, blaming, obsessive, narcissistic, ashamed, worried, despairing, disgusted, vengeful, paranoid, hopeless, helpless, indifferent, sorrowful, unworthy,* and *pessimistic.*

The most common attitudes that have a positive impact are: *enthusiastic, curious, friendly, humorous, hopeful, happy, joyful, cheerful, tolerant, passionate, hardy,* and *optimistic.*

Only Two Kinds of Attitudes

Robert Burton wrote a book in the early 1600s titled *The Anatomy of Melancholy*. At the time, this work wasn't widely received, nor was his theory accepted by his colleagues. He suggested that it wasn't emotions that caused illness, but attitudes. Burton believed that the release of a bad attitude improved the functioning of the body, as well as healing the deeper underlying meanings behind the illness. He offered that there are only two kinds of attitudes: the ones that make us happy and the ones that make us sick.

An Optimistic Attitude

An optimistic attitude makes us happy and goes a long way in creating the life and health we desire. These people generally believe that good things will happen to them, rather than bad. They see others as basically being good and display more tolerance toward their fellow human beings. They believe every day is a new adventure, the future looks bright, and things will work out well for them. Optimists don't think that life is the luck of the draw; they believe in making it whatever they want it to be. They're active and use their time productively, rather than sitting around and lamenting about how awful things are and how everything is always going wrong. There's no pity party for the person with this attitude.

Optimists downplay their faults and focus on their strengths. They look for the silver lining behind every dark cloud. They're happy and cheerful, yet at the same time realistic about what they're capable of. Consequently, they put themselves in situations where they can feel good about themselves and their performance. They're open to change and focus on solutions rather than problems. They tackle challenges in a straightforward manner and see themselves in control.

Optimists don't blindly accept what other people tell them, especially in the case of a diagnosis. They'll do their own research to find their own answers. They believe that even when bad news is delivered, there's always a bright side and something good will come of the situation. People with this attitude:

- Practice mental management to ensure their thoughts are positive
- Have a favorable explanation for things
- Don't blame others for what happens to them
- Expect things to go their way
- See themselves as being in control
- Don't have a defeatist or fatalistic view of things
- Participate in life and seek to live it joyfully
- Display healthy self-esteem
- Don't give up when the going gets tough

A Pessimistic Attitude

A pessimistic attitude makes us sick. Those with this outlook are easy to spot in a crowd. They're the ones who are agitated, confrontational, and verbally abusive. They think that life and other people owe them for all of the bad things that have happened. Their attention is focused on problems rather than solutions, and if answers are offered, they're quick to dismiss them as unattainable. When confronted with a problem, pessimists don't even try to fix it. Instead, they just accept it and figure out how to live with it. They're emotionally volatile, have short fuses, are defensive, and always expect the worst. Such an attitude leads them to believe that others are out to get them and will, if given the chance, take advantage of them.

Pessimists relinquish control of their healing process to someone else. Consequently, they have very strong expectations of what physicians should do and become frustrated and angry when they aren't met. When diagnosed, these folks accept the findings without question and believe whatever they're told. They jump to conclusions and will dramatize their illnesses as a means of gaining sympathy or getting attention.

Pessimists view life as being just one darn thing after another. They'd rather abdicate control than take the initiative to help themselves. It's almost as though acting on their own behalf in order to get well is too much effort—it's easier to take pills than to change the attitude. From this perspective, everything is wrong or broken, and it's someone else's fault—and that person's responsibility to fix it. Pessimists overgeneralize their illnesses and allow those disorders to become their identities. They believe that they can never seem to do anything right, everyone is out to get them, and nothing will ever turn out favorably. Why should it? It hasn't in the past, so it won't now. People with a pessimistic attitude:

- Only think of themselves and are solely interested in their own needs

- Practice all or nothing thinking

- Label people and are quick to judge

- Focus on the negative and ignore the positive

- Personalize everything and focus on their emotional wounds

- Display low self-esteem

- Jump to conclusions and are close-minded

- Think they have all of the answers and are quick to point out when someone else is wrong

- Blame strangers, the government, their family, their co-workers, and global circumstances for everything bad that happens to them

- Accept no responsibility for who, what, or how they are

How Attitudes Affect Health

Nowhere else in human behavior is it easier to uncover someone's attitude than in their health and in how they deal with being ill, because attitudes never lie. Sure, we can put on a happy face or take on a courageous demeanor if we have to, but if our attitude doesn't fit that behavior, it will show up in our body. In fact, the way we view ourselves and our lives has such a strong influence over our health that physicians can actually predict which people have the higher predisposition to illness just based on their outlook.

Attitudes are the heaviest burdens our body can carry because they keep us chemically out of balance and build up tension among the mind, body, and soul. This shows up in the muscles, organs, glands, and the energy body and can even cause the immune system to turn on itself, leaving the body vulnerable to infections and chronic illnesses.

Health and a Pessimistic Attitude

Pessimistic attitudes work just like stress in the body, only they don't subside the way that stress does. They just keep us in a constant state of turmoil, clouding our thinking and agitating the physical self. The outcomes from being caught in the throes of attitudinal strain are headaches, lower-back problems, dental problems, chronic pain, and high blood pressure. If left unchecked, it could develop into diabetes, autoimmune disorders, and even cancer. In one study conducted at a large university, it was found that people with a pessimistic attitude not only suffered from more colds, the illnesses lasted longer and caused more severe symptoms. The conclusion of this study was that pessimists got sick more because they expected to and because they didn't take care of themselves.

The area of the body where a pessimistic attitude shows up the most is in the gastrointestinal tract. The common health-related issues include gastric ulcers, hiatial hernias, and gastroesophageal reflux disorder (GERD). In the case of gastric ulcers, a condition where the lining of the stomach and upper small intestines becomes irritated and perforated with holes, it was discovered that being negative contributed significantly to the amount of acid secreted. Looking at this from a psychological perspective, pessimism creates bitter thoughts, which produce a caustic outlook on life. In the body, it manifests as a deterioration of the stomach lining.

However, there's another reason why this area is more susceptible to the effects of a pessimistic attitude: It's associated with gut instincts, personal power, and self-confidence, all of which are undermined by such an outlook. People who are prone to gastrointestinal issues tend to experience chronic frustration and feel they lack the support needed in order to help themselves. They have trust issues and are afraid of being betrayed, a common comment when they think doctors, health-care providers, or hospital staff have let them down. Pessimists also suffer from anxiety disorders and battle depression. Psychologically, they've lost their self-confidence.

One research study after another consistently shows how a pessimistic attitude affects health, not only contributing to the formation of illness, but actually shortening life spans. Most important, these studies show that if someone believes that bad things are going to happen, they usually do.

Health and an Optimistic Attitude

Since attitudes are learned behavior, we can change pessimism into optimism if we decide to, and one of the greatest motivators to help us in the decision is illness. A growing body of scientific evidence is showing that being positive not only promotes good health, it can actually be used as a preventive measure against getting sick in the first place. How? It builds up the immune system, making it easier for it to protect us against external factors. It also seems to speed up the healing process.

One of the illnesses that has consistently shown how an optimistic attitude helps in the healing process is cancer. It seems that people with this outlook participate more in their own recoveries. They display a stronger fighting spirit, handle the side effects of chemotherapy better, get better quicker, and in the case of terminal cancer, outlive those who are pessimistic about their chances of survival. Oncologists are recognizing that when people believe they can heal themselves and maintain an upbeat attitude, they do indeed recover.

The optimists refuse to give up or just sit back and let someone else determine their fate. They're willing to try different treatments and are open to new ideas. They invest the time to research the cancer and explore the options that can improve their odds. They refuse to let illness limit their lives and don't create an identity around it.

Studies showed other areas where an optimistic attitude paid off in the healing process: recovery time following surgery or an accident. People with an optimistic attitude were immediately making plans for what they were going to do when they got better, and did something every day that would expedite their healing progress. They meditated, used guided visualization, prayed, or said affirmations. They understood how powerful the mind is and created healing thoughts directed at their desired outcome. They knew the combination of healing thoughts and an optimistic attitude were better than any pills they could take.

There's also the connection between optimism and longevity. People with this attitude are more inclined to live healthier lifestyles and take better care of their bodies. They monitor their thoughts and manage their stress, making it a point to take downtime daily to calm their mental chatter. They focus on the prevention of illness; and if they should become unwell, they take a proactive posture rather than a passive one. And you'll rarely find them avoiding how they feel. They know if they don't take care of the body, it won't take care of them. They eat right, get the rest they need, do some form of exercise every day, and take the time to do the things that make them happy. Sounds pretty easy, doesn't it? All it takes is an optimistic attitude.

Peeling Away the Layers of Illness

Uncovering the contributors of illness is like peeling away the layers of an onion. We have to start on the outside with the things that are most easily recognized and then work our way to the center. The most recognizable outer layer is our behavior. It gives us a quick glimpse into our attitudes and tells us where we are mentally, emotionally, energetically, and physically—with the emphasis on physically, because the body can't hide things like the mind can. If we're doing or saying something that's compromising us, it will show up in our tone of voice and words and as physical stress.

Once we address the behavioral changes, then we're ready to peel away the next layers. However, it gets a bit trickier because we're into the realm of attitudes, beliefs, and emotions. It's much more difficult to release them— after all, they're tied to our identities and hold within them our emotional wounds. Letting go of them may make us cry, feel bad about ourselves, or be too harsh. In fact, when we reach the point of dealing with the contributors behind illness, we might even find ourselves asking some difficult questions: *Do we really want to let them go? Do we have to release or change them in order to get better? Can't we just stop at altering behavior but continue to retell our stories and remain comfortable within our belief systems? Or better yet, can we ignore them and hope they'll go away on their own?*

If we look at illness from the mind's perspective, we can do all that because we've been conditioned to ignore these deeper layers. From the physical perspective, we can forget about further work until the pain relievers, radiation, and chemotherapy no longer work. We might even be able to pull it off from the psychological perspective if we continue to suppress our emotions or until the antidepressants disengage us from the joys of life. However, what we can't do is pretend that none of the contributors exist or avoid changing what we need to when we have a psychospiritual perspective of illness. That's where we discover how all of the different aspects are connected and how they build off each other until they reach an unhealthy mental and physical state. At this point, we fully come to understand how the soul, mind, and body are inseparable and that what affects one, affects the others. It's from this perspective that we find the courage to dig deeper and to uncover the final layer—core themes, the body's powerful messengers.

CHAPTER 9

Core Themes: The Body's Powerful Messengers

Congratulations for sticking with the process and remaining steadfast in your desire to understand why we become ill! This chapter uncovers the deepest of all the hidden contributors and the ones that have the strongest hold over what we think, say, and do: core themes. Their grip is so strong that they can even override the intentions of the soul.

If we stepped back from our life for a moment, we'd see that it's merely a series of events that seem random and unconnected at the time we experience them, yet are very important. However, they really are connected because each event builds off the others emotionally so that they not only form our attitudes and beliefs, they create our core themes. These reveal the stories of our lives and strongly influence our behavior. Just think—every event, perception, drama, trauma, relationship (both the good and bad ones), fear, belief, success, and failure are rooted in our core themes. They're all just waiting for the right time and opportunity to resurface and express themselves through our words, actions, and health.

In addition to the core themes we create for ourselves, we're also gifted with those of our parents, grandparents, great-grandparents, great-great-grandparents, and so on. Yes, there are genetic core themes that are passed down from generation to generation. These tend to center around illness predispositions; economic status; levels of education; cultural and family traditions; religious beliefs; and expectations associated with being the first born, a middle child, or the youngest. They, too, are an integral part of our life stories and surface in our words and actions. However, for the most part we aren't even aware of these because they become entrained in our thinking and behavior at such an early age. Consequently, we just accept them as part of who we are, when they really don't belong to us at all. The only times we become aware of them are when they show up in our health.

Other than our inherent personality traits, core themes drive most of what we do and how we think and feel. However, they aren't always in alignment with who we really are. Perhaps we need to use emotional judgments to help us in the decision-making process, and that may require us to express how we feel about something before we can act on it. Yet if we've been conditioned to believe that acknowledging how we feel is bad and creates faulty decisions, we're going to find ourselves at odds with who we truly are. This will not only cause indecision and confusion, it will create a core theme of feeling inadequate because we can't seem to make good choices like everyone else.

Core themes are the composite of emotions, attitudes, and beliefs. They're the substructure behind our stories and are responsible for how we view life. They're like closets in our mind, where we lump everything together based on appearances. Every experience that has a similar emotional charge goes into the emotional part of the closet, and every thought that becomes fixed in a memory goes into the belief section. Yet if we were to look closer at the contents of our core-theme closets, we'd find they aren't the same at all. Using this analogy, some are shirts, some are blouses, some are skirts, and some are pants. The fact is that some core themes are ours, some belong to others, most are limiting, many have emotional hurts attached to them, and all are unhealthy because of how they affect both our mental and physical states.

When core themes surface and trigger old emotional hurts, it's difficult to understand the purpose they serve, yet they actually have several important functions. One is to form a mental blueprint that the brain can use to hasten the process of connecting a new experience with the past. Another purpose is aiding the mind in categorizing the constant stream of information it receives energetically and through the physical senses. Core themes offer the direction needed to help us navigate our way through all of the thoughts we create and the experiences we attract. They tell us what behavior is acceptable and what isn't and how we should interact with other people. They help steer us away from experiences and relationships that may cause us pain. Most important, they vividly show us what we need to change if we're to create the life and health we desire.

We're on an evolutionary journey that takes us through various stages and attracts many experiences, all intended to help us grow personally, evolve spiritually, and connect with our souls—to teach us how to live joyful and purposeful lives. Yet somewhere along the way, we've forgotten those intentions, because something else is driving us and causing us to disconnect from ourselves. When our core-theme closets are energetically filled with drama and trauma and charged with strong negative emotions, it's easy to see how we can lose touch with ourselves. It's apparent how we fall victim to our fears and allow them to determine who we are and how we live. We understand why we experience fear-based illnesses such as allergies, ulcers, strokes, asthma, hypertension, heart attacks, depression, autoimmune disorders, and cancer.

How Core Themes Express Themselves

Core themes are the motivation that drive our behavior. While they can be either negative or positive, most of the time the ones we deal with are negative because they're the ones that ultimately impact our health. They express themselves through our fears, which show up in how we interact with other people. As a matter of fact, anxieties and detrimental core themes are so intimately intertwined that it's difficult to tell them apart. Both create an obsessive and/or compulsive behavior, distort our thinking, create emotional blocks, compromise who we are, form distorted memories that are stored in the mind and body, and keep us from healing.

Core themes also express themselves through feelings, emotions, attitudes, and beliefs, for these are the reasons behind why we create core themes in the first place. Each one of these represents the progression of a thought before it becomes entrained in our behavior. If we were to look at these factors as the building blocks of our behavior, it would be much easier for us to change the negative core themes that are feeding our fears. How? All we would have to do is stop the process at any one of the contributors. For example, we could shift our emotional reaction to an old familiar situation. Rather than screaming and lashing out as we did before, we could take a deep breath and calmly excuse ourselves. We could also change our attitude about an experience. In the case of illness, instead of reinforcing our status with a pessimistic comment, we could say to ourselves, *Okay, I have a chance to change what's not working.* Or we could stop the progression by changing a belief. Again, in the case of being sick, rather than having the belief that someone else must heal us, we can have faith in healing ourselves. Better yet, we could stop the progression when a thought is still a feeling by adding a positive emotional charge rather than a negative one. Then fear wouldn't run our lives, love would. We'd be in control, rather than our core themes.

How Core Themes Develop

Jamie was taught very early in life the world was a hostile place because he grew up in the ghettos. All of the doors had multiple locks, and the windows had bars on them to keep the bad people out. Every night he lay in bed, afraid of the gunshots and screaming, and prayed that nothing bad would happen to his family and himself. He was afraid to walk to school because of the street bullies. He was scared of riding the school bus because of the fights and would cry or become frustrated and angry when someone accused him of initiating the altercations. All he wanted to do was become invisible so that no one could see him, talk to him, or hurt him. He just wanted to avoid a world that had become, in his mind, inhospitable and unforgiving.

As a result, Jamie built a core theme that fed his fears about rejection and confrontation, which he connected with hostility. Even as an adult, he wouldn't put himself in any position where he could experience antagonism. He was labeled antisocial because he wouldn't interact with others unless he absolutely had to. He wouldn't try anything new because he was afraid that he'd disappoint people and they'd become angry with him. He wouldn't engage in any competitive events, even though he loved playing basketball, because the coach or a fan might yell at him. His whole perception of reality and of himself had become so distorted by his core theme that it was affecting not only his life, but also his health.

That's the reason Jamie came to see me. He knew that he had to make some changes because he was sick and tired of living in fear. He knew that all of this had something to do with his chronic stomach problems and specifically with irritable bowel syndrome (IBS). I confirmed his suspicions by sharing how the stomach area of the body is associated with our personal power centers and how we hold the fear of rejection, betrayal, and the future in our stomachs and mid-backs. I let him know that IBS was the result of the suppressed emotions of resentment, disappointment, and self-directed anger. And I gently pointed out that his perception that the world was hostile was literally eating him up.

Jamie followed up with me several months later to tell me that his stomach problems were gone. When I asked him what he'd done, he said that he took what I'd shared in our session and began working with a psychotherapist to learn how to change his behavior and let go of the fears that were eating him up. He decided to get back into the game of life and be in control of it—rather than life being in control of him.

To help understand how core themes develop, here are a few examples, beginning with Jamie's. I've also included some suggestions of how to change them.

Experience: Interaction with other people

Feeling: I live in a part of town that's unsafe.

Emotion: It's a hostile environment.

Attitude: If my environment is hostile, then the world must be hostile.

Belief: I'm not safe anywhere I go, in any situation, or around people.

Core theme: I'll avoid any situation where there may be conflict.

Changing the core theme: In Jamie's case, he chose to seek the help of a mental-health-care professional because he knew that trying to make such changes alone would be too difficult.

Experience: Relationship with mother

Feeling: My mother avoids me when I don't do what she wants, and she tells me she doesn't love me when I don't behave.

Emotion: Her avoidance hurts my feelings and makes me sad.

Attitude: I'm a bad person, therefore no one will love me.

Belief: I'm not worthy of being loved.

Core theme: I'm a victim.

Changing the core theme: In this situation, begin by eliminating any negative self talk. Then change the attitude to: *I am a good, caring, and loving person.* Use this as an affirmation that you say every time you feel the victim persona surfacing. Find where in the body you're holding this negative attitude and then breathe love into the area and visualize the harmful charge dissipating. You'll actually feel a difference in this body part.

Experience: Workplace

Feeling: Thinking about work makes me anxious because I may not be skilled enough to do what's expected of me.

Emotion: Fear—I'm afraid of being fired.

Attitude: Who am I kidding?

Belief: Food stops the fear and makes me feel safe.

Core theme: I eat to feel safe.

Changing the core theme: In this situation, begin by changing the belief that food stops the fear. Take some classes that can help develop the necessary skills and that will focus the mind on something other than eating. Set up a strict meal schedule, including light snacks, and eat only at these times. Feeling safe has to do with being in control of your life, environment, and body.

Experience: People ignore me.

Feeling: When I'm talking to others, they walk away—especially when I'm discussing something serious.

Emotion: I'm afraid of the consequences of what I say.

Attitude: If I'm quiet, no one will be upset with me or think I'm stupid.

Belief: Others don't want to hear what I have to say.

Core theme: I have no voice; I'm silent.

Changing the core theme: In this situation, begin by altering the negative emotional charge around self-expression. Look at joining an organization that will teach you how to use your voice effectively so that people will want to hear what you have to say. This will build your self-confidence about speaking up. Or you can tell someone who walks away while you're talking how it hurts your feelings. Set some healthy boundaries for what's acceptable behavior and what's not, and then voice them.

Living through our emotional wounds and self-defeating core themes is certainly fraught with pain and suffering and definitely creates major stumbling blocks as we try to move forward in our evolutionary journey. Nevertheless, in the development of the human psyche, these obstacles represent the opportunity to transform the core themes that don't serve us well and to transmute the hold they have on us mentally and physically. If we're willing to let go of them and create positive core themes, the rewards are a positive attitude and good health.

How Core Themes Affect Health

Core themes are like viruses. Once they get into the mind and body, they're hard to get rid of and can lie dormant until the right environment brings them to life. This is a good metaphor to help understand how core themes work and how they contribute to the formation of illness. As with viruses, they aren't living organisms. They're merely distorted memories, so they rely on a host—emotions—to keep them alive. Once they have this support, they feed on themselves until they take over our behavior. At the same time they're changing the way we act, they're finding additional, similar emotions that will feed them so that they can multiply until the mind is overwhelmed and the body becomes ill. Both viruses and core themes weaken the immune system, with the former causing the system to turn on itself and the latter turning us against ourselves. The end result is the same, as both take their toll on our quality of life.

The problem with negative core themes is their insidious nature and how they cause low-grade anxiety, as if we're always waiting for the next bad thing to happen. This feeds the body an unending flow of stress hormones that eventually weaken its defenses against infectious diseases such as the common cold, flu, and various herpes viruses. Another problem with core themes is that because of their repetitive nature and strong emotional charge, they tend to weaken the parasympathetic part of the nervous system responsible for calming the body in an emergency. Basically, it's the *What if* and *If only* beliefs that keep the residual effects of core themes active and the nervous system in a state of alert.

Core themes also tend to be at the root of many of the chronic aches and pains we experience, especially in the neck and shoulders, the "carrying the weight of the world" location, and the lower back, the place of worry and deep-seated resentment. They're also tied to chronic illnesses such as arthritis, fibromyalgia, allergies, asthma, lupus, gastrointestinal disorders, thyroid disorders, diabetes, migraines, and hypertension.

The Key to Good Health Is Understanding the Contributors Behind Illness

These charts provide an overview of the psychological contributors to illness. Individually, they show how these factors impact our thinking and affect the body. Collectively, they reveal the progression of each one building off the others and the way they're all responsible for the core themes that influence our behavior.

FEELINGS
No contribution to illness

- Provide data without emotional judgment
- Are a source of input, both external and internal
- Rely on physical senses and intuition for information
- Help us understand the meaning of our experiences
- Provide insight into where we are mentally
- Assist the brain in sorting through the barrage of data it receives
- Offer different perspectives of situations or experiences
- Reveal repetitive patterns of thinking
- Assist the mind in the collection of data
- Create awareness
- Have no effect physically

EMOTIONS

*Contribute to dis-ease in the energy
body and weaken the immune system*

- Provide information with judgment attached to it—good or bad, right or wrong

- Rely on five physical senses for direction in how to react

- Reveal how external experiences are affecting us internally

- Offer insight into the quality of thoughts

- Alert us to personal compromise

- Assist the brain in its association and connection process

- Instantaneously change the physiology of the body

- Promote the release of endorphins with positive reactions; release stress hormones with negative reactions

- Support repetitive patterns of behavior

- Affect us physiologically and psychologically

ATTITUDES
Affect emotional state

- Are the result of learned behavior

- Alter our emotional outlook on life

- Reflect conditioning and social pressures

- Create redundant patterns of emotional reactions

- Are focused externally toward experiences and other people

- Impact self-perception and self-confidence

- Pessimistic attitudes:

    – Are thoughts reflecting emotional hurts

    – Form from suppressed emotions

    – Create apprehension, worry, and nervousness

- Optimistic attitudes:

    – Aid in the healing process

    – Inspire and foster hope

    – Create a fighting spirit

- Affect us psychologically

BELIEFS
Affect mental state

- Are formed from thoughts, emotions, and attitudes
- Limit perspectives of life
- Inhibit individuality
- Create core themes
- Lead to mental barriers
- Distort memories
- Form habits and comfort zones
- Reflect conditioning
- Encourage sticking with what's tried-and-true
- Are resistant to change
- Reinforce attitudes
- Create false self-perception
- Affect us psychologically

CORE THEMES

Contribute to chronic and life-threatening illnesses

- Support fears and beliefs
- Are a source of information, externally and internally
- Create fixed behavioral patterns
- Alter our emotional outlook on life
- Perpetuate limited thinking
- Reflect conditioning and other people's perceptions
- Impact interaction with others
- Produce insidious and prolonged changes in physiology
- Reinforce beliefs
- Attract experiences and individuals who support our beliefs
- Establish false values
- Impact self-expression
- Affect us physiologically, psychologically, and spiritually

---

Healing the Human Psyche

If you desire to truly heal yourself, then you must commit to being actively involved in the process rather than looking to someone else to do it for you. You must understand how your psychology affects your biology and address the mental and biographical contributors, as well as the physical factors responsible for the formation of illness. You must dig deep to uncover the emotions, attitudes, beliefs, and core themes that are preventing you from having the life and health you desire. Once you find them, you must be willing to release them. Begin by changing what you feel you have control over and seek help when you find yourself unable to proceed.

Invest the time and energy to gather the tools and techniques that will help you change your emotional reactions so that you're no longer held prisoner by old hurts. Practice mental management by shifting beliefs before they become core themes. Let go of all attitudes that say you're too old, too set in your ways, too emotionally wounded, or too ill to help yourself. Learn to use your feelings as they're intended—neutral inner messages sent by your soul and intuition that are rich with information, offering a different way to look at the same old thing. Most important, listen to your body because it will always give you an accurate read on where you are mentally and physically at that precise moment. If you're not where you want to be, change one thing. It really doesn't matter what you choose, because what affects one aspect of your being will have an impact on others.

If you're serious about turning your health around, get and stay involved in the healing process—even when you're feeling better. Achieving and sustaining well-being is an ongoing effort. It's a way of thinking and a lifestyle that mean maintaining a positive attitude.

When looking at what it takes to heal ourselves, I think Confucius stated it simply:

> *Tell me, and I will forget;*
> *show me, and I will remember;*
> *involve me, and I will understand.*

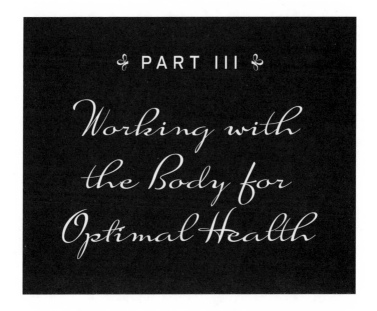

❧ PART III ❧

Working with the Body for Optimal Health

"He who advised a sick man, whose manner of
life is prejudicial to health, is clearly bound first
of all to change the patient's manner of life."
— Plato

"Health is not valued until sickness comes."
— Thomas Fuller

"Like any other major experience, illness actually changes us.
How? Well, for one thing we are temporarily relieved from the
pressure of meeting the world head-on. . . . We enter a realm of
introspection and self-analysis. We think soberly, perhaps for the first
time, about our past and future. . . . Illness gives us the rarest thing
in the world—a second chance, not only at health, but at life itself."
— Louis E. Bisch

"I find that my spirits and my health affect each other
reciprocally that is to say, everything that discomposes my
mind, produces a correspondent disorder in my body; and
my bodily complaints are remarkably mitigated by those
considerations that dissipate the clouds of mental chagrin."
— from The Expedition of Humphrey Clinker by Tobias Smollett

CHAPTER 10

How the Body
Cries Out for Help

This part of the book is where we begin to apply all that we've learned about the hidden contributors behind illness. Rather than exploring them theoretically, we'll connect them with the structure and functioning of the physical body in a way that will make the information practical and usable.

The body, besides being the vehicle our soul uses to find physical expression, is a well-engineered, precise, self-regulating healing machine. It's designed with all kinds of diagnostic equipment—such emotions and hormones—to let us know where it is at any point. It also comes equipped with self-repairing features—such as the immune system, energy system, and endocrine glands—that will naturally restore it back to proper functioning, as long as nothing interferes with the process. It has within it a myriad of check-and-balance systems to cancel out the effects of stress and emotional distress so that it can remain healthy. Yet, this doesn't always happen. Why? We're so busy *being busy* that we don't take the time to listen to the messages. Instead, we'd rather ignore them and hope they'll go away on their own—or better yet, fix themselves. And even when we do become aware of those bulletins, we're not sure what to do because we don't know how to read what they're trying to tell us.

In addition to all of the other features of the human body, it's also a highly sophisticated communication system transmitting and receiving a constant flow of information via the mind/body connection. The exchange is both energetic and electrochemical and travels to its intended receiver via the central nervous system, considered by metaphysicians to be the lifeline between the mind, body, and soul. When the body sends messages, it's asking for help. It's trying to call our attention to the fact that something externally or internally is affecting its functioning, and if that isn't changed, it could potentially cause harm. It's asking us to act on the problem—to fix it or eliminate it immediately. Since thoughts are at the root of everything we do, it's easy to see how unhealthy thinking over time can wear the body down, thus leaving it susceptible to the formation of illness.

The body knows when our health is headed in the direction of a chronic or serious disorder long before the mind does, and its job is to avert that. When the body experiences the initial indicators that something is wrong, which shows up as pre-illness in the energy body, it will begin the process of alerting the mind. However, at this point there's no reason to cause the brain to overreact and flood itself with fearful, consuming thoughts that would immobilize its ability to move into action. So the body sends different messages to indicate the degree of malfunction and the urgency needed to deal with the problem. If we learn how to decipher the different messages, we'll find that they not only tell us where the problem is in the physical structure, they reveal the underlying psychological contributors responsible for the trouble and even let know us what we need to do to restore the mind and body back to good health.

Physical Messages

When the problem is affecting the physical state, the body will use symptoms to direct our attention to what it needs. An example of this is migraine headaches. Since they certainly cause acute head discomfort and affect the sensitivity of the eyes, it would seem logical for a doctor to examine the brain to ensure there's nothing seriously wrong neurologically, such as a tumor. However, if we looked at some of the other symptoms of migraines, we'd see that they're also accompanied by nausea. Using the body's messages, we find that it's trying to tell us that the issues in the stomach are affecting the brain and preventing it from functioning effectively. It's alerting us to a chemical imbalance, perhaps pH or stress hormones, that are compromising the vascular system. It's revealing they're having an impact on the brain's ability to think clearly, so it's unable to identify and fix the problem. The body and mind are fixated on the head, where many of the symptoms are, but the root cause is in the stomach and solar plexus.

Other physical messages the body sends can take form as fatigue, muscle tension, stress headaches, aches and pains, syndromes (clusters of symptoms), chronic disorders, and life-threatening illnesses.

Psychological Messages

When the mental and emotional states are affecting the physical, the body will use metaphors, symbolism, and dreams to alert us that something's causing psychological distress, which is disturbing the functioning of specific areas such as the heart, the liver, the kidneys or the digestive tract.

Metaphoric messages create images in the mind to help it in the association and connection process. In doing so, the mind is able to see what it must change if the body is to restore itself to proper functioning. An example of this kind of message might be an image of us as children feeling sad when we were scolded for doing something bad. In this case, we're being told that there are emotions, beliefs, and perhaps even core themes that are buried deep in that memory—and those factors are impacting our health. The images combined with the emotional charges are causing us to relive how we felt. They're reminding us that we're no longer children, so we can let go of the reactions. This will keep them from continuing to compromise the body.

By reliving the memory, we're able to identify that the emotional charge is sadness, and we can actually feel it in specific parts of the body. If we find sadness in our heart, the message is alerting us that if we don't let go of the emotion, it could potentially weaken the heart until it breaks. "Broken heart" is the metaphor for myocardial infarction, or heart attack, and the emotion of sadness is energetically stored in the left ventricle, where such attack occurs.

In the case of symbolic messages, we find ourselves experiencing something externally, yet connecting and relating to it internally. An example is agoraphobia, a mental disorder involving fear of leaving safe surroundings.

When someone is worried about personal safety and security, and it has mentally immobilized them to the point that they're housebound, it will eventually affect their health because of the constant onslaught of stress hormones, and specifically the elevated levels of cortisol. In this situation, the messages bring attention to the fact that the mental state is affecting the physical. However, within a symbolic message, the body is also offering the opportunity to heal the problem by making it obvious so that the mind can act on what it needs.

Here is how this message works:

1. It heightens the person's awareness of the physical surroundings.

2. It increases the activities of the physical senses.

3. It engages the brain's reticular-activating system to assist in the recognition of external consistencies.

If the person believes they need to see police officers everywhere they go in order to feel safe, their brain will accommodate this by focusing their attention on the presence of the police. Eventually, they'll feel safe enough mentally and emotionally to release the fear, and their body will return to its proper functioning.

Dream messages reveal the hidden meanings behind our illnesses without having to engage the conscious mind, which is notorious for creating a flood of fearful thoughts that compound the physical effects. In the dream state, there aren't emotions such as worry; there's only information. An example of how the dream message works can be seen in the case of a woman with a breast lump. When this is discovered, the conscious mind is fixated on the lump itself and preoccupied with constantly questioning whether it's benign or cancerous. The longer the woman waits to get her answers, the more consuming the fear becomes, until the body and mind become so mentally and emotionally exhausted that neither can function properly.

Then in a dream, she sees that the lump isn't cancerous, but instead is a ganglion cyst. It's showing how storing anger and disappointment is forming this little toxic dump site holding these emotions in the breast area. In this situation, the woman wakes up the next morning and finds that the fear surrounding the lump is suddenly gone and her mind is no longer preoccupied with its presence. Later, if the diagnosis validates the dream, the conscious mind is ready to work on letting go of these emotions because it recognizes how harmful they are.

If we're to effectively learn how to read the messages the body sends us, then it would be helpful if we had a better understanding of how this magnificent healing body works.

The Essentials of the Human Body

Most of us have a natural curiosity about our body and are interested in learning more about how it works, why it becomes ill, and what can be done to assist in the healing process. Our curiosity began as infants when we explored our bodies with our hands and stared at the movements of our hands and feet. As we grew older, we wondered where food went when we swallowed it, what caused us to go to the bathroom, and why we changed as we entered into puberty. As adults, our focus shifted from curiosity to problem solving. Instead of marveling at our physical capabilities, we want to know what we can change to eliminate hot flashes or heart disease. We want to know why our metabolism changes with age, why our digestive tract doesn't work the way it did when we were younger, why we have trouble sleeping, and what we can do to bring our body back to the flexibility and health we had when we were in our 20s and 30s. Our focus changes from curosity to prevention, and rather than taking our body for granted, we become almost obsessed with taking care of it so it will take care of us.

Knowing the essentials of how our body is put together: its *anatomy,* and how it works: its *physiology,* is the first place to start. By learning about these elements, as well as *homeostasis,* we'll gain an understanding of how the organs, glands, and all the systems are completely interdependent, not only for proper functioning, but also for the body's survival. We'll begin to comprehend how thoughts, emotions, attitudes, beliefs, and core themes affect the different parts of the body and why they can be so destructive to our well-being. And we'll get how important it is for everything to function optimally if we're to experience good health.

The word *homeostasis* describes the body's tendency to sustain a relatively stable internal balance through the coordinated efforts of organs and systems, even when external situations, circumstances, and conditions are challenging it. While the literal translation is static—a combination of *homeo,* meaning the same and *stasis,* meaning standing still—the term doesn't really mean that the functioning of the body is unvarying. After all, we know it has to change if it's to adapt to its external and internal needs. Rather, homeostasis refers to a state of balance in which internal operations are shifting only within narrow margins so that the overall functioning won't be compromised. When the body works homeostatically, all organs, glands, and systems interact efficiently, thus maintaining the needs of the internal environment.

However, when the needs of the body aren't met and/or it's subjected to chronic bouts of stress or emotional distress, then the internal functioning falls outside of the margins of change, and homeostasis is compromised. In effect, the parts lose their ability to communicate effectively with one another. The result takes form in the messages of aches, pains, muscle tension, discomfort, stress, emotional distress, and ultimately illness.

In preparation for learning where emotions, attitudes, fears, and core themes are mapped in the body, let's take a closer look at the physical structure and how each part functions.

— **Cells** are the product of specific molecules being combined. One of the smallest units of all living things, they not only have their own individual jobs, they're an integral component of the functioning of every part of the human body. Although no two cells are exactly alike, they all do have the same basic parts: the nucleus, which holds genetic material, and the plasma membrane, a transparent barrier that contains the cell's contents and separates it from the surrounding environment. *Cells are where we energetically store soul memories, recollections with emotional charges, and core themes associated with life events, experiences, and situations.*

— **Tissue** consists of groups of similar cells that share a common function. There are four primary types of tissue: epithelial, connective, nervous, and muscle. When combined, they form the fabric of the body.

- *Epithelial tissue* is the lining, covering, and glandular tissue of the body. Glandular tissue forms the various glands in the body. This type has no blood supply of its own and depends on connective tissue for food and oxygen. If well nourished, it will remain healthy and regenerate itself. *This is one of the places where we energetically store emotions, specifically fear.*

- *Connective tissue,* as its name implies, links body parts. It's found everywhere and is the most abundant and widely distributed of the tissue types. It's subdivided into two categories:

  1. Rigid: bone, cartilage, and dense connective tissue (tendons, ligaments, and the lower layer of skin)

  2. Soft: loose connective tissue and blood

  This is one of the places where we energetically store beliefs, and this tissue serves as the connection between beliefs, core themes, and behavior.

- *Nervous tissue* receives and conducts electrochemical impulses from one part of the body to another. It's wound-healing matter because it stimulates the body's inflammatory and immune-system responses. It also works with the other tissues to aid in the healing process. *This is one of the places where we energetically store core themes.*

• *Muscle tissue* is highly specialized to stretch and contract; it produces movement. The different types include skeletal, cardiac, and smooth. Skeletal tissue pulls on the bones and skin to create movement and is controlled voluntarily. Cardiac tissue contracts the heart and is controlled involuntarily. Smooth tissue is found in the walls of the stomach, bladder, uterus, and blood vessels. This, too, is controlled involuntarily. *This is one of the places where we energetically store emotions.*

— **Organs** are composed of two or more tissue types, and each organ performs a specific function that is both independent of and interdependent on other organs. At this level, extremely complex functions become possible. For example, the small intestine is responsible for the digestion and absorption of foods and is comprised of four different tissues. Each organ has a job to do, and all of them working together helps maintain the homeostasis of the body. *This is one of the places where we energetically store emotions and attitudes.*

— **Glands** consist of one or more cells that make and secrete a particular product called hormones. There are two kinds of glands:

- *Exocrine:* These have ducts through which secretions empty into the epithelial tissue surface. They include sweat glands, oil glands, and the liver and pancreas. *These are some of the places where we energetically store emotions.*

- *Endocrine:* There are seven ductless endocrine glands in the body: pineal, pituitary, thyroid, thymus, adrenal, pancreas, and reproductive organs (ovaries and testes). There's also an eighth gland, the spleen, where metaphysicians believe all self-directed anger is energetically stored. *These are some of the places where we energetically store emotions and attitudes.*

— **Systems** are groups of organs that cooperate to accomplish a common purpose. They make it possible for the body to function in a synchronized manner. A system reveals the physiology of the body, meaning how it works. An example is the digestive system, which includes the esophagus, stomach, small and large intestines, and rectum. When all of these components work together, they keep food moving so that it's properly broken down for absorption into the blood, providing fuel for all of the cells.

Here are the major systems in the body:

- The *integumentary system* is the skin, which waterproofs the body and cushions and protects the deeper tissues from injury. It secretes salts and urea in perspiration and helps regulate body temperature. Receptors for temperature, pressure, and pain alert us to what's happening externally. This system contains the neurohormonal pores that receive energy-carrying information externally; it's also part of the vascular autonomic system. *It's through the skin that every thought, emotion, and attitude is externally received before being transmitted to the nervous system for distribution.*

- The *skeletal system* consists of the bones, cartilage, ligaments, and joints. It supports the body and provides the framework that the skeletal muscles can use to cause movement. It also has a protective function in supporting the organs. *This system stores beliefs, fears, and core themes.*

- The *muscular system* has only one function and that is to facilitate movement. These muscles differ from those of the heart, which are cardiac, and other hollow organs, which are intended to move fluids. *This system stores emotions.*

- The *nervous system* is the body's fast-acting main control system. It consists of the brain, spinal cord, nerves, meridians, sensory receptors, five physical senses, and neurohormonal pores in the skin. It responds to both internal and external changes by activating appropriate muscle nerve trunks, organs, and glands. It includes these systems: central nervous, autonomic, vascular autonomic, and sensory. *This system stores core themes.*

- The *endocrine system,* like the nervous system, controls the body's activities, but it acts much more slowly. It secretes hormones that regulate processes such as growth, reproduction, and metabolism. It includes the pineal, pituitary, thyroid, thymus, and adrenal glands, along with the pancreas, the ovaries in females, and the testes in males. The glands of this system aren't connected anatomically in the same way that the parts of the other organ systems are. They're controlled by secretions rather than electrochemical impulses. *This system stores emotions.*

- The *cardiovascular system* consists of the heart, arteries, veins, and vessels. It's responsible for transporting blood rich in oxygen, nutrients, hormones, and other substances to all parts of the body. It also removes waste such as carbon dioxide, toxins, bacteria, and dead or cancerous cells. *This system stores emotions and attitudes.*

- The *lymphatic system* assists the cardiovascular system in removing unwanted waste and protecting the body from intruders that could potentially cause it harm. It consists of lymphatic vessels, lymph nodes, the spleen, and tonsils and is crucial to the immune response. It's also responsible for returning fluid leaked from the blood to the vessels so that blood can be kept continuously circulating through the body. *This system stores attitudes. The body's immunity or lack of it is primarily dependent on either an optimistic or pessimistic outlook on life.*

- The *respiratory system* sees that the body is continually supplied with oxygen, while at the same time removing carbon dioxide. It consists of the nasal passages, pharynx, larynx, trachea, bronchi, and lungs. The gaseous exchanges occur through the walls of the air sacs in the lungs. *This system stores emotions, attitudes, and core themes.*

- The *digestive system* is basically one continuous tube running through the body from the mouth to the anus. Its role is to break down food and deliver its by-products to the blood for assimilation into the cells. Any undigested matter is eliminated through the bowels. Components include the mouth, esophagus, stomach, small and large intestines, and rectum. The liver and gall bladder are also considered part of this system. Although it's also part of the endocrine system, the pancreas delivers digestive enzymes to the small intestine, so it, too, is included here. *This system stores emotions, beliefs, and core themes.*

- The *urinary system* produces waste and then removes it from the body via the kidneys, ureter, bladder, and urethra. Another important function is maintaining the body's water and salt balance and regulating the acid-based balance of the blood. *This system stores emotions.*

- The *reproductive system* consists of the ovaries (female) and testes (male) and is part of the endocrine system. *This system stores emotions, specifically fear and love; beliefs; and core themes. It has a major impact on our self-perception and our interactions with other people.*

The Body Still Needs Our Help

In addition to all of its self-monitoring, self-regulating, and self-repairing features, the body has an innate self-sustaining capacity, meaning that it can continue to function even when parts are removed or not functioning properly. For example, the liver can still function when more than two-thirds of it are destroyed. (In fact, other than the skin, the liver is the only organ that will regenerate itself if a portion is removed or damaged.) A person can live a fairly normal life with one lung removed, as long as the other lung is functioning properly. The immune system can continue to do its job fighting off and killing invaders even when the spleen, an integral part of the system, is removed. In the case of a stroke, if a small portion of brain tissue is destroyed, the brain will find other neurological pathways to compensate for the damage. And even when people experience heart attacks, they can continue to live long, full lives.

With its ability to recover from strokes, heart attacks, and even cancer, the body still can't seem to heal the hidden psychological contributors that slowly and insidiously eat away at it and wear it down to the point of destroying it. As magnificent as it is, the body still needs our help in removing all of the contributors—mental, emotional, and physical—that are responsible for its breakdown. We must decode its messages and pay attention to where it's experiencing pain, discomfort, and illness. It still needs us to act on its messages the second we receive them and not ignore them until things escalate to something more serious.

Most important, our body still needs us to change patterns. All we need to know is where to look for them.

CHAPTER 11

Mapping the Hidden Contributors of Illness in the Body

The psychospiritual approach to healing requires that we eliminate all of the contributors preventing the body from functioning properly. This means we need to remove the emotions and attitudes held in the organs, glands, and muscles and the fears, beliefs, and core themes held in the spine and nervous system. This would be easy if we knew precisely where to find them wouldn't it? The mapping charts in this chapter will help provide that information.

It's important to remember that the intention of every experience is to move us forward on our evolutionary journey. Keep in mind that we're always making progress, even when we think we're not. We're never stuck, only our thoughts become blocked when we repeat them in our behavior. Illness is a reflection of such thinking; it doesn't mean that we've lost momentum. Specific illnesses are the natural physical outcome of certain thoughts and emotional reactions lingering in specific parts of the body.

Here's an example of how the mapping process works, how it can help uncover the hidden contributors of illnesses, how it can help us understand the messages the body's sending, and how to use the information to begin the healing process.

Diabetes is the result of an improperly functioning pancreas, the organ that holds the emotional charges of grief, sadness, and hatred. The pessimistic attitudes stored there are low self-esteem, helplessness, bitterness, and hopelessness. In the case of diabetes, the metaphoric message of the body is that you've lost the capacity to have a joyful life, your passion for the things that are important to you, and the sweetness in life.

Taking this information, you're now ready to start applying it to the healing process. You can begin by connecting what you've learned with a memory charged with grief, sadness, and hatred—a childhood recollection that caused you to feel helpless and suffer from low self-esteem. Once the memory and emotions have been identified, you're ready to change them. Don't worry about changing the attitudes; they'll naturally shift when you take away the emotions feeding them.

Ask yourself, *What emotions can I create that will cancel the negative ones?* Switch grief to pleasure, sadness to happiness, and hatred to love. To ensure that the old emotions and attitudes don't resurface in the pancreas, cease feeding the sadness with sweets. Instead, do something that makes you happy, something you love to do.

The History Behind the Mapping Charts

The mapping charts are the result of more than 15 years of studying, researching, observing, and interacting with hundreds of people who came to me for medical intuitive readings. What I discovered early on in my work was that illnesses had their own patterns of psychological contributors, no matter the personality type, age, ethnic origin, or individual conditioning. The body's messages around specific disorders were consistently the same as to how they affected specific parts of the body. I would always find fear in the right atrium of the heart, bladder, reproductive organs (both male and female), and spinal plexus. I would always find anger in the right ventricle of the heart and liver, and when self-directed, in the spleen. Because the organs, glands, and systems are all connected and interdependent on each other, I would find a consistency in beliefs and core themes throughout the body and discovered that they fed each other based on emotional charges.

However, the information in the mapping charts isn't inclusive. I only charted the strongest emotional expressions, those that appeared to have the greatest impact on the body's functioning. There are numerous possibilities, as there are numerous different people. The same holds true for fears and core themes: I only mapped the top ones. Keep in mind that the intention behind sharing these charts is to help you start the process of uncovering the hidden contributors behind illness so you can begin the healing process by removing them. Remember, healing happens with your help.

Helpful Hints for Applying the Mapping Charts Information

The best approach to using this information is just that: to see it as information. Should you decide to dig deeper into your psychological coffers, I suggest that you work with a trained mental-health professional, doctor, or member of the clergy. If you're experiencing any aches and pains, have discomfort in any parts of the body listed in the charts, or have been diagnosed with an illness, you can use your intuition to see if the information I've shared is applicable to your situation.

There are several ways to apply the information. You can begin by identifying symptoms and becoming aware of where you're experiencing them—but symptoms aren't the origin of the problem. They're just the escalated expression that has moved to another part of the body and finally gained the attention of the mind. For instance, thrush in the mouth is a symptom; the origin site is the small intestine in the form of candida. So you'll want to learn about any symptoms, trace them back to where they started, and then uncover the contributors in that part of the body.

Second, if you become ill or experience symptoms, it's helpful to look back at least three days prior to your noticing something was amiss, because it's usually within that time period that your body started sending its subtle messages that something isn't right. What was happening in your life? Were you under a lot of stress? Did something upset you, such as an argument or an event rooted in a fear? Ask yourself if what you experienced was an old familiar pattern or another "been there, done that" situation. If so, get a clear read on the emotions you were feeling and the thoughts going through your mind. Was someone else involved in the situation? Was the person male or female? Did it remind you of something you experienced as child—perhaps something associated with your mother or father? All of your answers will provide insight into why you're dealing with these problems and what you can do to heal them.

Listen to the words you're using when describing your illness or your symptoms. Don't own them or identify with them, for words symbolize what's happening in the body. For instance, if you say, "My boss is a pain in the neck," do you have a pain in the neck? If you declare, "Doing that makes me sick to my stomach," do you have stomach problems? Or if you snap, "I'm so irritated with myself," are you experiencing a cold, skin rashes, a herpes virus outbreak, or gallbladder issues? The metaphors we use to explain how we feel affect us physically.

Finally, ask yourself *What is the illness or symptom preventing me from doing?* What would you be accomplishing if you weren't sick? These questions usually reveal the origin site of the problem and uncover the beliefs and core themes associated with that part of the body. Remember that beliefs and core themes create distorted self-perceptions. So if you find yourself thinking about what you'd do if you weren't ill (like walking), there's a very good chance that the symptom sites are in your feet or knees and the origin is somewhere in your lower back. That's where the fear of unknown is stored with the core theme of lack of control.

If we step back and listen to what we say and what our body is communicating and eavesdrop on our thoughts, the process of uncovering the hidden contributors behind symptoms and illness is really very logical. However, unlike our conditioning has led us to believe, if we have to choose between logic and emotions . . . emotions will always win.

Mapping Emotions and Attitudes in the Major Organs (Anterior View)

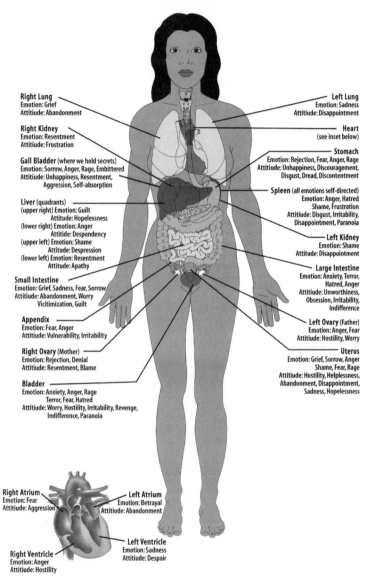

Right Lung
Emotion: Grief
Attitude: Abandonment

Right Kidney
Emotion: Resentment
Attitiude: Frustration

Gall Bladder (where we hold secrets)
Emotion: Sorrow, Anger, Rage, Embittered
Attitiude: Unhappiness, Resentment, Aggression, Self-absorption

Liver (quadrants)
(upper right) Emotion: Guilt
Attitude: Hopelessness
(lower right) Emotion: Anger
Attitude: Despondency
(upper left) Emotion: Shame
Attitude: Despression
(lower left) Emotion: Resentment
Attitude: Apathy

Small Intestine
Emotion: Grief, Sadness, Fear, Sorrow
Attitiude: Abandonment, Worry
Vicitimization, Guilt

Appendix
Emotion: Fear, Anger
Attitiude: Vulnerability, Irritability

Right Ovary (Mother)
Emotion: Rejection, Denial
Attitude: Resentment, Blame

Bladder
Emotion: Anxiety, Anger, Rage
Terror, Fear, Hatred
Attitiude: Worry, Hostility, Irritability, Revenge, Indifference, Paranoia

Left Lung
Emotion: Sadness
Attitiude: Disappointment

Heart
(see inset below)

Stomach
Emotion: Rejection, Fear, Anger, Rage
Attitiude: Unhappiness, Discouragement, Disgust, Dread, Discontentment

Spleen (all emotions self-directed)
Emotion: Anger, Hatred Shame, Frustration
Attitude: Disgust, Irritability, Disappointment, Paranoia

Left Kidney
Emotion: Shame
Attitude: Disappointment

Large Intestine
Emotion: Anxiety, Terror, Hatred, Anger
Attitude: Unworthiness, Obsession, Irritability, Indifference

Left Ovary (Father)
Emotion: Anger, Fear
Attitude: Hostility, Worry

Uterus
Emotion: Grief, Sorrow, Anger Shame, Fear, Rage
Attitiude: Hostility, Helplessness, Abandonment, Disappointment, Sadness, Hopelessness

Right Atrium
Emotion: Fear
Attitude: Aggression

Left Atrium
Emotion: Betrayal
Attitiude: Abandonment

Left Ventricle
Emotion: Sadness
Attitude: Despair

Right Ventricle
Emotion: Anger
Attitiude: Hostility

Organ	Emotions	Attitudes
1. *Lungs*		
(right lung)	Grief	Abandonment
(left lung)	Sadness	Disappointment
2. *Heart*		
(upper-right atrium)	Fear	Aggression
(lower-right ventricle)	Anger	Hostility
(upper-left atrium)	Betrayal	Abandonment
(lower-left ventricle)	Sadness	Despair
3. *Stomach*	Rejection	Unhappiness
	Fear	Discouragement
	Anger	Disgust
	Rage	Dread
	Hostility	Discontent
4. *Gall Bladder*	Sorrow	Unhappiness
(Where we hold secrets)	Anger	Resentment
	Rage	Aggression
	Bitterness	Self-absorption
5. *Liver*		
(upper-right quadrant)	Guilt	Hopelessness
(lower-right quadrant)	Anger	Despondency
(upper-left quadrant)	Shame	Depression
(lower-left quadrant)	Resentment	Apathy
6. *Spleen*	Anger	Disgust
(all self-directed emotions)	Hatred	Irritability
	Shame	Disappointment
	Frustration	Paranoia
7. *Kidneys*		
(right kidney)	Resentment	Frustration
(left kidney)	Shame	Disappointment
(both kidneys)	Dread	Despair

Organ	Emotions	Attitudes
8. *Large Intestine*	Anxiety	Unworthiness
	Terror	Obsession
	Hatred	Irritability
	Anger	Indifference
9. *Small Intestine*	Grief	Abandonment
	Sadness	Worry
	Fear	Victimization
	Sorrow	Guilt
10. *Appendix*	Fear	Vulnerability
	Anger	Irritability
11. *Bladder*	Anxiety	Worry
	Anger	Hostility
	Rage	Irritability
	Terror	Revenge
	Fear	Indifference
	Hatred	Paranoia
12. *Uterus*	Grief	Hostility
	Sorrow	Helplessness
	Anger	Abandonment
	Shame	Disappointment
	Fear	Sadness
	Rage	Hopelessness
13. *Right Ovary*	Rejection	Resentment
(Mother)	Denial	Blame
13. *Left Ovary*	Anger	Hostility
(Father)	Fear	Worry

Mapping Emotions and Attitudes in the Endocrine Glands (Anterior View)

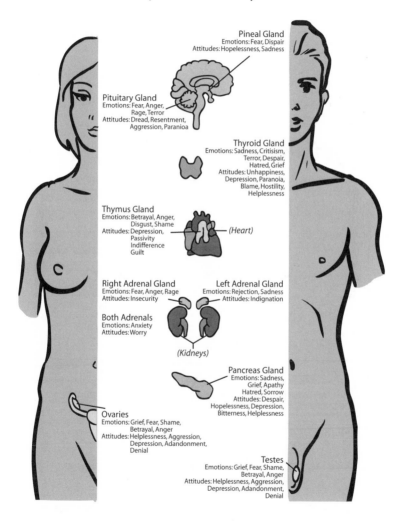

Pineal Gland
Emotions: Fear, Dispair
Attitudes: Hopelessness, Sadness

Pituitary Gland
Emotions: Fear, Anger, Rage, Terror
Attitudes: Dread, Resentment, Aggression, Paranioa

Thyroid Gland
Emotions: Sadness, Critisism, Terror, Despair, Hatred, Grief
Attitudes: Unhappiness, Depression, Paranoia, Blame, Hostility, Helplessness

Thymus Gland
Emotions: Betrayal, Anger, Disgust, Shame
Attitudes: Depression, Passivity Indifference Guilt

(Heart)

Right Adrenal Gland
Emotions: Fear, Anger, Rage
Attitudes: Insecurity

Left Adrenal Gland
Emotions: Rejection, Sadness
Attitudes: Indignation

Both Adrenals
Emotions: Anxiety
Attitudes: Worry

(Kidneys)

Pancreas Gland
Emotions: Sadness, Grief, Apathy Hatred, Sorrow
Attitudes: Despair, Hopelessness, Depression, Bitterness, Helplessness

Ovaries
Emotions: Grief, Fear, Shame, Betrayal, Anger
Attitudes: Helplessness, Aggression, Depression, Adandonment, Denial

Testes
Emotions: Grief, Fear, Shame, Betrayal, Anger
Attitudes: Helplessness, Aggression, Depression, Adandonment, Denial

181

Gland	Emotion	Attitude
1. *Pineal*	Fear	Hopelessness
	Despair	Sadness
2. *Pituitary*	Fear	Dread
	Anger	Resentment
	Rage	Aggression
	Terror	Paranoia
3. *Thyroid*	Sadness	Unhappiness
	Criticism	Depression
	Terror	Paranoia
	Despair	Blame
	Hatred	Hostility
	Grief	Helplessness
4. *Thymus*	Betrayal	Depression
	Anger	Passivity
	Disgust	Indifference
	Shame	Guilt
5. *Adrenals*		
(right gland)	Fear/anger/rage	Insecurity
(left gland)	Rejection/sadness	Indignation
(Both)	Anxiety	Worry
6. *Pancreas*	Sadness	Despair
	Grief	Hopelessness
	Apathy	Depression
	Hatred	Bitterness
	Sorrow	Helplessness
7. *Testes/Ovaries*	Grief	Helplessness
	Fear	Aggression
	Shame	Depression
	Betrayal	Abandonment
	Anger	Denial

Mapping Emotion in the Back Muscles
(Posterior View)

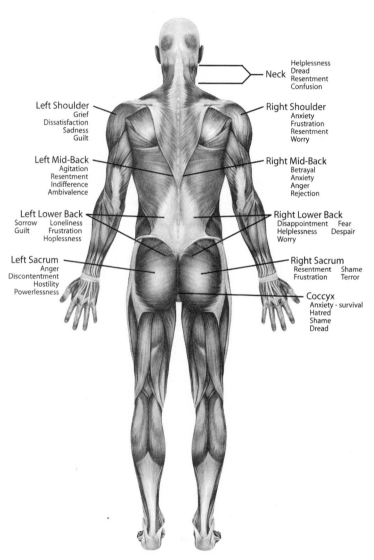

Neck
Helplessness
Dread
Resentment
Confusion

Left Shoulder
Grief
Dissatisfaction
Sadness
Guilt

Right Shoulder
Anxiety
Frustration
Resentment
Worry

Left Mid-Back
Agitation
Resentment
Indifference
Ambivalence

Right Mid-Back
Betrayal
Anxiety
Anger
Rejection

Left Lower Back
Sorrow   Loneliness
Guilt   Frustration
Hoplessness

Right Lower Back
Disappointment   Fear
Helplessness   Despair
Worry

Left Sacrum
Anger
Discontentment
Hostility
Powerlessness

Right Sacrum
Resentment   Shame
Frustration   Terror

Coccyx
Anxiety - survival
Hatred
Shame
Dread

Area	Center	Right Back	Left Back
Neck	Helplessness		
	Dread		
	Resentment		
	Confusion		
Shoulders		Anxiety	Grief
		Frustration	Sadness
		Resentment	Dissatisfaction
		Worry	Guilt
Mid back		Betrayal	Agitation
		Anxiety	Resentment
		Anger	Indifference
		Rejection	Ambivalence
Lower back		Disappoint-ment	Sorrow
		Helplessness	Hopelessness
		Worry	Guilt
		Fear	Frustration
		Despair	Loneliness
Sacrum		Resentment	Anger
		Frustration	Discontentment
		Shame	Hostility
		Terror	Powerlessness
Coccyx	Anxiety—survival		
(Tail bone)	Hatred		
	Shame		
	Dread		

The Spine . . . Lifeline of the Soul, Body, and Mind

Most people experiencing pain, discomfort, symptoms, or illness will turn to others for help. It was no different thousands of years ago. However, the metaphysicians in ancient times diagnosed and treated illness much differently, even though today we suffer from many of the same conditions created by the same causes. Rather than using symptoms, as is today's approach, they identified a person's mental state to determine treatment. They believed that the only enemy of the body and health was the quality of thoughts, and when the outer world overtook the thoughts of the inner world then illness would be the outcome. Therefore, they began by relieving the person of unhealthy ideas and then moved to treating the body.

The metaphysicians also took a different diagnostic approach in locating the origin of illness. Whereas medicine today looks at the organs and glands and their functioning, they examined the spine. They considered it the lifeline of the soul, mind, and body, and believed illness was the result of some form of disconnection in the spinal nerve trunks or some restriction in the flow of spinal fluid. They thought that the spine would reveal not only where the disconnection was occurring, it would also show the underlying causes of it.

The Spine

The spine is a flexible column consisting of 33 vertebrae that form the trunk that connects the head with the body. The metaphysicians associated the human trunk with that of the Tree of Life, which represents how the soul, mind, and body are all one and how all interact, thus making it possible for all aspects of humanity to communicate with each other and evolve simultaneously. As a result, their perception of illness was that any damage to the trunk would result in harm to the communication process. This is what they referred to as the disconnection.

The vertebrae are basically bones stacked one on top of the other forming a ladder that's hollow inside, thus protecting the spinal cord and the fluid that runs through it. The metaphysicians believed the spinal cord was the manifestation of the soul in the physical body and the fluid was the life source of the soul. Unlike contemporary or Chinese medicine that divides the spine into five groups, the metaphysicians saw six groups and believed that within these they could uncover the contributors responsible for illness. The names of the six groups were assigned because of the positions they occupied in the body:

1. *Atlas,* the first vertebrae of the cervical spine
2. *Cervical,* 6 in number
3. *Thoracic,* 12 in number
4. *Lumbar,* 5 in number
5. *Sacrum,* 5 in number
6. *Coccyx,* 4 in number

They considered the coccyx to be the most rudimentary part because it's believed to ground the soul into the physical body. They also saw the thoracic spine as a sort of mirror reflecting the thoughts created in the outer world. Consequently, they began their diagnostic process in this section to see if there was a disconnection and then worked their way up the spine to see if the thoughts had caused a break with the soul, or they worked down the spine to investigate whether there was a damaged link with the body. It was a very effective way to determine the cause of illness.

Everywhere throughout the history of medicine, there are writings revealing how the spine was considered to be an effective tool in determining the nature of illness and how it could be used to uncover both the physical and psychological contributors. Even today, in the field of chiropractic treatment, a minor adjustment to the spine can alleviate any disconnection that may be keeping the mind, body, and soul from being able to work together in a cooperative, unified manner.

The Ritberger Body Mapping™ Diagnostic Process of Using the Spine

My diagnostic process of using the spine to unover the hidden contributors behind illness involves several givens:

- The nature of the body is to always seek a state of homeostasis, and it will do so if it can stay within its narrow margins.

- The cause of illness is associated with thoughts, emotions, attitudes, beliefs, and core themes that become fixed in our memories, thus creating unnatural and compromising behavior.

- There are six fears, common to all people:

  1. Survival
  2. The unknown
  3. Abandonment
  4. Betrayal
  5. Rejection
  6. Dying

  These are interrelated and are the source of all aberrations and of other fears.

- The bones of the body store beliefs and core themes.

- The spine is divided into six groupings and each one can be associated with fears, core themes, and basic beliefs.

Here's a mapping chart combining all of these factors in order to identify the origin of illnesses, their nature, and the hidden contributors behind them.

The Six Primary Fears and Their Locations in the Spine

Atlas: fear of dying
Cervical: fear of rejection
Thoracic: fear of betrayal
Lumbar: fear of abandonment
Sacrum: fear of the unknown
Coccyx: fear around survival

The Six Primary Fears and Their Location in the Spine

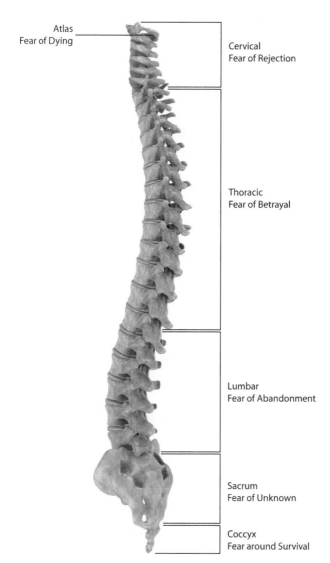

Atlas
Fear of Dying

Cervical
Fear of Rejection

Thoracic
Fear of Betrayal

Lumbar
Fear of Abandonment

Sacrum
Fear of Unknown

Coccyx
Fear around Survival

The Six Primary Core Themes
and Their Locations in the Spine

Atlas: lack of joy
Cervical: not accepted
Thoracic: not supported
Lumbar: not loved
Sacrum: lack of control
Coccyx: lack of security

The Six Primary Core Themes and
Their Location in the Spine

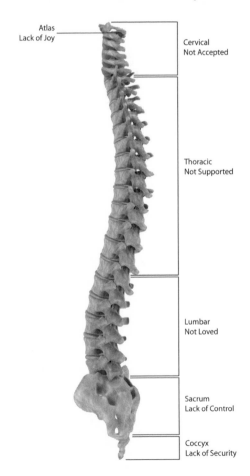

Atlas
Lack of Joy

Cervical
Not Accepted

Thoracic
Not Supported

Lumbar
Not Loved

Sacrum
Lack of Control

Coccyx
Lack of Security

Beliefs and Their Correlation to the Core Themes

*This list of beliefs isn't intended to be inclusive.
It's just a sampling of how core themes support
individual beliefs. There are as many beliefs as there
are expressions of emotion and different types of people.*

Location	Core Theme	Beliefs
Atlas	Lack of joy	Life's hard.
		Life's a struggle.
		I hate my life.
		I feel stifled.
		I'm stuck.
		I'm sick and tired.
		I'm so lost.
		Will I ever get it?
		What about my needs?
Cervical	Not accepted	I'm bad.
		I have no self-worth.
		I worry about what others think of me.
		I try, but it's never good enough.
		Nobody appreci-ates me.
		All I would like is for people to listen.
		I'm not like every-one else.
		No one likes me.

Location	Core Theme	Beliefs
Thoracic	Not supported	I help everyone else, but nobody helps me.
		It's my job to be responsible and solve problems.
		If I don't, who will?
		Nobody listens to what I have to say.
		I have a hard time trusting others.
		I try to help, but people don't value it.
		I would rather be alone than be with someone who doesn't care.
		I'm tired of doing everything myself.
Lumbar	Not loved	I'm inadequate.
		I'm no good.
		I can love others but not myself.
		Nobody loves me.
		I'm destined to be alone.
		Will I ever have a relationship?
		I'm emotionally wounded.
		All I want is to be loved.
		Every time I love someone, they leave me.

Location	Core Theme	Beliefs
Sacrum	Lack of control	There's too much to do and too little time.
		I'd better get my house in order.
		Other people are always telling me what to do.
		I'll never get to where I want to be.
		I resent people wasting my time.
		My life is full of clutter.
		I need to take care of unfinished business.
		I'm always a day late and a dollar short.
Coccyx	Lack of security	I'd better save for a rainy day.
		You never know when you'll need it.
		People will steal from you if you give them half a chance.
		The only things you can count on are death and taxes.
		Something bad usually happens.
		My life is filled with scarcity.
		I can barely make ends meet, even if I work hard.

Beliefs and Their Correlation to the Core Themes

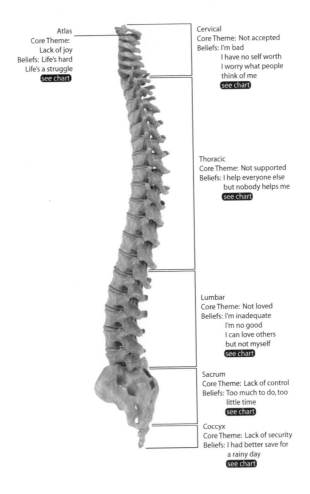

Atlas
Core Theme:
Lack of joy
Beliefs: Life's hard
Life's a struggle
see chart

Cervical
Core Theme: Not accepted
Beliefs: I'm bad
I have no self worth
I worry what people
think of me
see chart

Thoracic
Core Theme: Not supported
Beliefs: I help everyone else
but nobody helps me
see chart

Lumbar
Core Theme: Not loved
Beliefs: I'm inadequate
I'm no good
I can love others
but not myself
see chart

Sacrum
Core Theme: Lack of control
Beliefs: Too much to do, too
little time
see chart

Coccyx
Core Theme: Lack of security
Beliefs: I had better save for
a rainy day
see chart

Using the Mapping Chart of the Spine

Illness is an evolutionary process that takes time to develop. It just doesn't happen overnight, even though that's what we think when we recognize the first symptoms that something isn't right. Illness also has three phases: an origin site, a primary symptom site, and a secondary symptom site. For the most part, we're usually unaware of the first one, because the messages it sends fall beneath the threshold of our physical senses. Instead, they surface energetically and emotionally.

The primary symptom site is where we first become aware there's a problem because we experience some discomfort, tension, aches, or pains that capture our attention. Depending on the degree of discomfort, the mind will either fixate on the symptoms or ignore them. If for any reason it chooses to ignore the messages—perhaps the discomfort level isn't severe enough—the secondary symptom site comes into our awareness. However, at this phase the illness has moved beyond just the minor troubles, and the mind and body are alerting us that things have progressed to the point that we need to act on them. By the time illness evolves through all three phases, the overall well-being of the body has been compromised, and we experience the first pangs of fear.

Each of these sites is also associated with the three aspects of our being: the soul, mind, and body. And each of them has different needs for being restored to good health. The origin site is associated with the soul, the primary symptom site with the mind, and the secondary symptom site with the body. In order for healing to happen, the origin site must be identified first and its needs met. Working on the symptom sites without addressing where they came from is like putting a little bandage on a large open wound. It will be hard to heal in the necessary way.

Mapping the Spine Exercise

Taking this information, let's use the mapping chart of the spine to help us find the origin site of an illness. Here are some clues: The origin site is where we'll find our *chronic* issues, whether it's in the body as a *chronic* weakness or problem, in the mind as a *chronic* fear, or in the soul as a *chronic* core theme which prevents it from finding its physical expression through our experiences. The key word around the origin site is *chronic.* It's also where our soul will use our intuition to alert us that something's not quite right, either through an inner knowing, a premonition, or our dreams.

Let's use chronic lower-back problems as an example origin site and use the mapping chart of the spine to uncover the hidden meanings behind this disorder. The lumbar spine is where you hold the *fear of abandonment* and the core theme *not loved.*

Ask yourself, *Would I prefer to stay in a bad relationship rather than not have one at all? Am I afraid that people will leave me if they find out who I really am? Is low self-esteem or low self-worth something I struggle with? Am I worried about what others will think about me or whether they'll like me? Is anxiety an ongoing problem for me? Do I always feel as though I've done something wrong when anyone gets upset?* If you answered yes to most of these questions, then there's a very good probability that the underlying contributors behind the weakness in your origin site is the *fear of abandonment* and the core theme is *not loved.*

Okay, now what? Ask yourself which one you want to begin working on—the fear or the core theme. Once you make that decision, write it down. Next, list everything you can change to make it go away. Write down one thing you can do right now and do it. Then do the same thing the next day and the next for at least ten days straight. Next, repeat the process, identifying something else you can do. Here's another clue: Affirmations and guided visualizations are very effective tools for facilitating the shift, and they remove the emotional charges attached to fears and core themes.

Here's how the process would look:

What do I want to work on? Not feeling loved

What are the things I can change? I can stop worrying about what people think of me. I can volunteer my time to help others. I can learn to love myself. I can create a statement to say to myself every time I find myself not liking who I am.

What can I do right now? Create an affirmation: *I love me and celebrate who I am.* I will say this every time I find myself feeling bad about myself or not liking who I am.

That wasn't hard, was it? The really exciting part about this process is that the minute you say this affirmation, the energetic disconnection between the soul and the body will be repaired and the flow of fluid in the spine will become unobstructed, as will the energy-carrying information running through the nervous system. After the third or fourth day, your mind will reorganize itself to accept this input as the truth and will begin the process of releasing the old negative core theme and replacing it with a positive one.

Around this same time, you'll start to notice that your feet don't hurt as much or your legs don't seem to get as tired or as restless, and the knots in the muscles in your shoulders will relax or go away. Why will you notice a change in these spots? They're the areas that are the primary and secondary symptom sites for the origin site of the lumbar spine.

How to Use All of the Mapping Charts

Each of the charts is intended to help you uncover the potential hidden meanings behind your aches, pains, and illnesses and to offer insight into what you can do to heal yourself. Since getting better requires attention and intention, the charts will help you decide where you want to begin the process: mentally, emotionally, physically, or spiritually. However, I must reiterate once again the importance of seeking help. If you're displaying any of the psychological patterns listed on any of the charts and are dealing with an illness, I recommend that you seek the services of a doctor, a mental-health professional, or a holistic practitioner. I'm such a firm believer in creating a healing team because it's difficult for us to step back and remain emotionally detached enough that we can get a complete picture of what's going on and have a clear understanding of what we need to do if we're to truly heal ourselves. If nothing else, it helps to have someone to discuss our fears with.

Even physicians—and many have seen me for a session—will be the first to tell you that it's a lot easier to heal if you aren't being held hostage by your fears. The spine-mapping chart will help you identify your "mother of all fears," and the other charts will assist you in identifying the different psychological contributors feeding that fear. Armed with this information, you're ready to identify the needs of the soul, mind, and body and to associate each of them with specific common illnesses.

❧ ✤ ❧

CHAPTER 12

Common Illnesses and Their Hidden Meanings

There are three basic needs we all have in common no matter what our gender, age, conditioning, or personality type:

1. To grow and express ourselves
2. To connect with other people and feel loved
3. To feel secure and in control of our lives

Whenever any of these needs aren't being met, either individually or collectively, illness is the outcome. It's that simple.

Yet uncovering why there's a lack takes time, and when we're dealing with an illness, just aren't feeling well, or are mentally overwhelmed, we don't always feel we have the time to stop and try to figure out the reasons. This is when a doctor, therapist, medical intuitive, or holistic practitioner can help. However, as I've discussed throughout this book, these individuals really can't heal us. The best they can do is to help us understand why we aren't getting what we need and offer suggestions for how we can. It's then up to us to do the work.

Knowing that illness is the result of any of these three needs not being met makes it easier to home in on what we need to do in order to heal ourselves. In fact, it takes everything in this book to the next level. How? First of all, it reduces illness to three categories:

1. The needs of the soul: to grow and express itself

2. The needs of the body: to connect with other people and to feel loved

3. The needs of the mind: to feel secure and in control of life

Second, it provides a much needed short-term reprieve when the mind is overwhelmed and fixated on the symptoms of the body.

Sure, at some point in time we'll still need to dig into our psychological coffers to clean up the remnants of our past thoughts, perceptions, emotions, attitudes, beliefs, and core themes that are the root cause of illness to ensure they won't continue to resurface and affect our health and lives. However, classifying illnesses into one of these three categories not only shifts how we approach healing, but actually accelerates the process. Instead of having to spend time dredging up the past, now we can focus on discovering what we need to give to our soul, mind, and body so that all three will once again work in a cooperative healthy manner and homeostasis can be restored.

Here's a clue to help you expedite the process of uncovering the needs: *Be in the present moment, because only then will you become aware of what you need to change in order to give the soul, mind, and body what they need.*

What Illness Reveals

The illnesses listed in this chapter focus on the negatives in emotions, attitudes, beliefs, and core themes. These are the psychological contributors behind illness and are responsible for the three needs not being met. If the positives outweighed the negatives then our well-being wouldn't be compromised. Having stated that, a few disclaimers are in order.

It's important to note there's an element of illness that I haven't addressed in this book: genetics and how that factor increases the potential for illness, especially specific conditions such as diabetes, thyroid disorders, heart disease, strokes, and cancer. As you're looking at the contributors of illness, this certainly needs to be a top consideration. However, I believe that a family history of illnesses doesn't necessarily mean that you'll develop them. With the right preventive measures—both physical and mental—it's possible to not experience the same ailments as your relatives.

The following descriptions of illnesses and their psychological interpretations are *general in nature* and should be considered as a basic understanding of the hidden meanings behind the associated condition. Consequently, their descriptions may not directly match a symptom or a disorder that you're currently experiencing. Keep in mind that everyone is unique, so considerations have been taken to preserve and honor that. Rather than seeing the information as being inclusive and an absolute representation, see it as a starting place instead.

The descriptions aren't intended to define why we become ill or make us feel bad about ourselves. We all have dysfunctions because they're the nature of conditioning. In fact, I heard a quote once that summed it up perfectly: "Anytime we have interaction with anyone other than ourselves, there's bound to be dysfunction."

My intention behind presenting this information is to shift the perception of illness and help open the doorways of the mind so that we can catch a glimpse of what we're holding in our psychological coffers. Once those portals are open, it's up to each of us to decide what to do with the knowledge.

To do this, the following pages offer a general description of each illness, the psychological implications, the associated emotions, the needs behind the condition, and the changes necessary to remove the hidden meanings. The descriptions are written in a way that speaks to the inner healer within each of us. Just reading the information will connect us with the needs of the soul, mind, and body. Amazingly, sometimes that's all it takes to heal.

Asthma

General description: Asthma is an inflammation in the bronchial tubes triggered by allergens such as smoke, chemical toxins, animal dander, molds, and food additives. It can be activated by a cold, flu, stress, adrenal exhaustion, hypoglycemia, low thyroid, or high salt intake. It can also be set off by food allergies to wheat, corn, and dairy products.

Psychological implications: There's a tendency to worry and live with a low-grade level of anxiety that something bad is going to happen. When not fretting about the future, asthmatics tend to dwell in the past with all of the failures, bad times, and negative events that happened to them— and that support their need to worry. They tend to bury their emotions and are unwilling to express their needs. They create codependent relationships, yet become resentful and feel stifled—even smothered—by their partners. They look to others to make their decisions for fear of making bad ones, and then they resent the same people for trying to control them. They're sullen and feel guilty about almost everything. That's because they believe it's their fault when things go wrong.

Associated emotions: Grief, disappointment, resentment, anger, guilt, and shame

The needs behind the illness: Soul—to grow and to express ourselves

What to change: Attitudes

Autoimmune Disorders

General description: These are triggered when the mechanisms of the immune system become imbalanced. It reacts to normal body tissues as though they were allergens, thus making the body allergic to itself and causing the system to turn on itself.

Psychological implications: The root of any autoimmune disorder—whether it's chronic fatigue, lupus, rheumatoid arthritis, fibromyalgia, or AIDS—tends to be the psychological pattern of unrealistic self-expectations and self-directed anger. This is the kind of rage that causes people to be allergic to themselves and turn against themselves, much like illnesses that cause the immune system to turn against itself.

The individuals who tend to have the highest susceptibility to these disorders are those who are immobilized by self-doubt, who never seem to find the personal satisfaction and gratification they seek and crave, who feel like they never fit in conventional social structures, who have a fear of failure, who don't trust, and who are relentless in their self-criticism.

Associated emotions: Fear, anger, anxiety, frustration, shame

The needs behind the illness: Soul—to grow and express ourselves; mind—to feel secure and in control of our lives

What to change: Attitudes and thoughts

Candida

General description: Candidiasis is a fungus found in the intestinal tract that normally lives in a healthy balance with the other bacteria and yeasts found throughout the body. However, when the pH (acid and alkaline) gets out of balance, the conditions in the intestinal tract change and create the perfect environment for this fungus to multiply rapidly. Because of this, the immune system is weakened and its ability to maintain the fungus and bacteria balance is compromised. The result is candida, a yeast infection that can surface in the vaginal area or bladder or become systemic throughout the body and manifest as oral thrush.

Psychological implications: Candida reflects emotional distress over relationships, specifically with the mother. These people feel unsupported, unappreciated, and unloved. They become bitter and turn sour in their disposition. They're pessimistic and tend to blame others for the misfortunes in their life. They feel helpless, disgusted, and angry—both with themselves and those around them. Since the relationship with the mother is so important for emotional development, when there isn't a strong connection, there are intense feelings of inadequacy and a tendency toward addictions such as food, spending, and sometimes even gambling. These individuals use their addictions as a means of trying to fill the emotional emptiness they feel. They're also more susceptible to bouts of depression. There's a tendency to bury emotional hurts and deny themselves the pleasures of love or being in a caring relationship.

Associated emotions: Grief, sadness, sorrow, hatred, fear of abandonment

The needs behind the illness: Body—to connect with other people and feel loved

What to change: Patterns

Cancer

General description: Cancer is the mutation of a cell that has lost its normal control mechanisms, thus experiencing unregulated growth. It can form from any tissue within an organ. As the malformed cells grow at abnormal rates, they form a mass of cancerous tissue that invades adjacent tissue; cancer can also metastasize to other parts of the body. It's more likely to develop when the immune system isn't functioning properly.

Psychological implications: This is one illness where allopathic and behavioral medicine agree; both consider cancer to be the disease of nice people, meaning that there's a higher predisposition for it in those who suppress their feelings and emotional needs, who are inclined to avoid conflict at all costs (even at their own expense), and who tend not to make demands on anyone because they don't want to be seen as a burden or too needy. Cancer-prone personality types are those who tend to feel that they need to put the emotional needs of others before their own. While usually considered a desirable and admirable quality, self-denial tends to suppress the expression of emotions, personal needs, and desires. This type of behavior encourages martyrdom and supports the fears of abandonment and rejection. When asked why they want to heal themselves, one of the most common responses is that they want to be well for their spouse or their children. Rarely is it for themselves. It seems that even when their own mortality is threatened, they'll still put the needs of others before their own.

Associated emotions: Loneliness, hopelessness, helplessness, pessimism, resentment, powerlessness

The needs behind the illness: Soul—to grow and express ourselves

What to change: Attitudes

Chronic Fatigue Syndrome (CFS)

General description: Once considered primarily caused by the general fatigue that comes from overworking or prolonged bouts of stress, research now shows that this syndrome is actually the result of an autoimmune system disorder that interestingly affects more women than men. While not conclusive, it's believed that the cause is the Epstein-Barr virus, which is responsible for mononucleosis, as both share many of the same symptoms.

Psychological implications: The most common underlying cause associated with chronic fatigue syndrome is the frustration that comes from being mentally overloaded and never having the time to do what's important. Sufferers experience what Dr. Stephen Covey, the author of *The 7 Habits of Highly Effective People,* calls the "urgency addiction," meaning they're driven by the need to do what's pressing rather than doing what's important. Those with CFS consistently expressed that before their illness they felt that their lives were out of control, they were overscheduled, they experienced emotional numbness, and they seemed to run from one thing to another without ever having the time to enjoy life. They complained that people drained them of energy, always taking and never giving back. They didn't have the time to do what they loved. Instead, they spent their time responding to the demands of others. They suffer from what I call the "NO Syndrome," meaning the inability to say no when someone needs their help. They seem to have difficulty delegating tasks and responsibilities and believe that if they don't do things personally, nothing will be done right or on time.

Associated emotions: Anger, resentment, frustration, anxiety, irritability, fear of betrayal

The needs behind the illness: Mind—to feel secure and in control of our lives

What to change: Thoughts

Depression

General description: Depression usually occurs when there's a disruption in life's normal balance, a loss, conflict, or trauma, and rather than being a single illness or condition, it's believed to be the result of a group of mood disorders that strike with varying intensity. The medical cause is difficult to pinpoint, however if looked at psychologically, there are specific predictable thoughts and emotions.

Psychological implications: Sufferers' perception of the world is that people and life have let them down, and they have no one to support them emotionally. They feel alone and abandoned and display the behavior of being a victim of circumstances. They feel that they have no control over what happens to them. They are reactionary rather than being in charge of their journeys. They harbor the perceptions that everything is against them and being alive isn't all it's cracked up to be. Their world shrinks as they pull inward and their enthusiasm to engage in life may become nonexistent. Everything is a hassle, too difficult, or not worth the effort. They feel empty inside and void of emotions.

Associated emotions: Grief, sadness, sorrow, despair, helplessness, hopelessness

The needs behind the illness: Body—to connect with other people and feel loved

What to change: Patterns

Diabetes Mellitus

General description: This is a disorder in which the blood levels of glucose (sugar) are abnormally high because the body doesn't release or use insulin adequately. There are two types: type 1 and type 2, the most common. People with type 1 produce little or no insulin at all. In type 2, the pancreas continues to manufacture insulin, but the body develops a resistance to its effects, resulting in a deficiency. Obesity and family genetics increase the risk of type 2 diabetes.

Psychological implications: These individuals have a feeling that the sweetness of life is slipping away and their burdens are overriding their ability to enjoy it. This causes a tendency to look to other things to feed the discontentment they feel inside, which is food in many cases. Yet the foods that fill their psychological cravings aren't necessarily those that support the health of the body. The psychological roots underlying diabetes are associated with the feelings of lack—of passion, love, happiness, joy, abundance, hope, and the ability to find and enjoy simple pleasures. They tend to long for what was and live in the past. They express a deep dissatisfaction with life. In many cases, they believe that they don't deserve to have their needs met and see themselves as not being worthy of the pleasures that life offers. They feel bitter and unhappy, causing them to suffer from low self-worth and self-esteem.

Associated emotions: Grief, sadness, sorrow, guilt, worry, apathy, bitterness, hopelessness

The needs behind the illness: Soul—to grow and express ourselves; body—to connect with other people and feel loved

What to change: Attitudes and patterns

Fibroids

General description: Fibroids are noncancerous masses that grow in the lining of the uterus or in breast tissue. In the uterus, they're undetectable until they grow large enough to cause problems such as heavy menstrual bleeding. At that point, they can also cause abdominal and pelvic pain. In the breast, they're movable, rubbery nodules that surface as small lumps. Care for the liver can prevent the presence of fibroids.

Psychological implications: Fibroids are the toxic dump sites for self-directed anger, shame resentment, and disappointment. They're the holding place for old emotional wounds that feed fears of abandonment and betrayal. Strong feelings of inadequacy and not being good enough also exist. There are rejection issues with a parent: In the case of the mother, there's frustration over never being able to please her or gain her approval. For the father, there are avoidance issues along with a problem of being criticized for being too emotional, or he may have set up unrealistic expectations that created abnormal behavior. These people struggle with personal power issues and have a difficult time with worthiness. It seems that no matter how hard they try, it's never enough. It's as if they constantly have to prove themselves in order to gain the acceptance and respect they desire. They're perfectionists that set unrealistic expectations both of themselves and other people.

Associated emotions: Disgust, disappointment, anger, grief, sorrow, shame, rage, hostility

The needs behind the illness: Body—to connect with other people and feel loved

What to change: Patterns

Fibromyalgia

General description: Basically, fibromyalgia is an arthritic disease of the muscular system and its components: the fascia, which is a thin, clear, semiliquid substance that holds the muscles, nerves, and tissues together; the tendons, which attach the muscles to the bones; and the ligaments which attach the bones to each other. Most discomfort and pain associated with fibromyalgia occurs within the fascia, which is responsible for moving toxins and other unwanted waste substances out of the muscles and tissue for elimination.

Psychological implications: These people struggle with lack-related issues—lack of personal power, self-love, self-worth, competency, resources (both time and money), and support. They feel separated from the world, as if they're outsiders watching others with happy, healthy lives. They harbor deep-seated resentment and frustration because they can't seem to execute and manifest their desires and dreams. It's as if they're stuck, and no matter how hard they try, they can't seem to get ahead. Their perception is that life's a struggle and it's difficult. They tend to suppress their emotions and bury old emotional hurts. They feel trapped, either in a negative relationship or a bad job, and are afraid to take the steps necessary to change. They have difficulty staying grounded in reality. It's easier for them to view things through the lens of their imagination than to see them for what they really are. These folks easily become overwhelmed by the demands of life; they think it's hostile and people are unkind. They struggle with the violence and animosity of the world and can't understand why everyone can't just get along and accept each other rather than causing conflict and creating emotional pain. Rather than going with the flow, they're resistant; and rather than dealing with problems, they carry them around in the fascia of the muscles.

Associated emotions: Dissatisfaction, guilt, worry, helplessness, hopelessness, despair, disappointment

The needs behind the illness: Mind—to feel secure and in control of our lives; body—to connect with other people and feel loved

What to change: Thoughts and patterns

Heart Attack

General description: The blood supply is suddenly and severely restricted or cut off, causing the heart to stop functioning. The heart muscle dies from lack of oxygen if the supply of blood isn't quickly restored.

Psychological implications: These individuals live with constant and prolonged stress and display the classic type A behavior: high-strung, aggressive, demanding, and rarely satisfied. They need to be in control both of people and their environments. They seem to always be in competition with themselves and have difficulty accepting their weaknesses, setting unrealistic expectations and then pushing themselves to achieve their goals. They're angry, resentful, hostile, cynical, argumentative, and unrelenting in their pursuit of their goals and objectives. Their perception is that life is hard, it involves a lot of work, and getting ahead is a constant uphill battle. They experience frequent bouts of sadness and feel empty inside, as if life is passing them by. They feel put-upon and as though people take advantage of them. They harbor resentment for having to carry the responsibility of providing for others. They struggle with fears about survival and the unknown.

They tend to be skeptical and don't trust anyone—in many cases not even themselves. They never complain about being at loose ends, but instead claim that they always have too much to do. They long for a slower pace, a better quality of life, and the time to enjoy what they work so hard to accumulate. They express that they can't seem to find the love, support, or appreciation they need.

Associated emotions: Sadness, anger, resentment, fear, betrayal, hostility, despair

The needs behind the illness: Soul—to grow and express ourselves

What to change: Attitudes

High Cholesterol

General description: Cholesterol is a fat-related substance that's naturally produced by the body and is essential for normal functions such as creating new cells, insulating nerves, and manufacturing hormones. The liver is responsible for making all of the cholesterol the body needs. Genetics, poor metabolism, chronic inflammation, and overindulgence in artery-clogging foods contribute to elevated levels. There are two kinds of cholesterol: HDL or good cholesterol and LDL/VLDL or bad cholesterol. VLDL is responsible for transporting triglycerides—sugar-related blood fats which usually appear on the thighs and hips.

Psychological implications: These individuals are angry inside and have trust issues. They believe that people don't care about them and are just using them. They have insecurity issues about loss—of money, jobs, material items, and health. There's a tendency for cynicism, suspicion, prejudice, and paranoia. They're overly critical, judgmental, opinionated, and unrealistic in their expectations. They easily become angry, frustrated, and disgusted when others don't listen to their suggestions or do what they think is right. They're slow to forgive and tend to stew inside rather than expressing their emotions. They're prone to melancholy and bouts of depression. When in these states, they're "doom and gloom" people and have difficulty saying anything positive or see any goodness in the world. They focus on problems and dwell on them to the point of exaggeration. They have difficulty finding joy in life. They're high-strung, overly ambitious, overindulgent, overloaded, and overworked. They're rarely satisfied with where they are.

Associated emotions: Anger, guilt, shame, resentment

The needs behind the illness: Mind—to feel secure and in control of life

What to change: Thoughts

Insomnia

General description: Insomnia encompasses a variety of sleep disturbances such as difficulty drifting off, frequent awakenings, difficulty going back to sleep, and waking up too early.

Psychological implications: There are three major fears that contribute to insomnia:

1. Fear of the unknown (lack of control)
2. Fear around survival (safety and security)
3. Fear of abandonment (not feeling loved)

People with insomnia tend to struggle with trust issues, although more so with themselves than others. This creates an attitude of discontentment and unhappiness. Things are never right or the way they should be, or they never have enough, whether it's time or money. They're emotionally frazzled and easily become overwhelmed with details. They have a never-ending task list, and no matter how hard they try, they can never seem to get a handle on all that needs to be done. This monumental to-do list eats them up, which in turn weakens their immune system, leaving them vulnerable to chronic stress-related illnesses. Their common complaint is that they don't have balance in their life. Stress is the norm, and when they do have any discretionary time, they fill it up with chores rather than relaxation.

Associated emotions: Grief, fear, worry, resentment

The needs behind the illness: Mind—to feel secure and in control of our lives

What to change: Thoughts

Irritable Bowel Syndrome (IBS)

General description: This is a chronic inflammation where the membranes of the colon become irritated, causing abdominal cramps; sharp stabbing pains; or problems with constipation, diarrhea, indigestion, gas, bloating, belching, or nausea. Dietary changes are the best treatment.

Psychological implications: Stress is a major contributor to IBS, as is chronic worrying. Sufferers tend to be nervous and anxious about life. They have high expectations of themselves that they can never seem to meet, so there's always the element of disappointment. They're self-critical and have trouble digesting change. Fear of failure is paramount, and control is a big issue for them. They micromanage time, tasks, other people's activities, and even their own schedules because they're afraid that things will fall apart if they relinquish control. They're bossy, domineering, irritable, and difficult to please and can suffer from obsessive-compulsive behavior. Emotionally, they're unpredictable and can be moody, pensive, and volatile. It's difficult for other people to know what's going on with them because they're unwilling to share how they're feeling or what they're thinking. They push and push and can never seem to leave well enough alone. They can be confrontational and aggressive when unhappy with themselves.

Associated emotions: Frustration, worry, guilt, rage, anger, disappointment

The needs behind the illness: Body—to connect with other people and feel loved; mind—to feel secure and in control of our lives

What to change: Patterns and thoughts

Migraines

General description: A migraine is a headache that's characterized by throbbing, aching pain on one side of the head coupled with nausea, chills, vomiting, weakness, visual disturbances, and dizziness. They can be genetic or caused by food allergies, MSG, artificial sweeteners, hormone imbalances, weather changes, or a deficiency of serotonin.

Psychological implications: Sufferers tend to be overly ambitious, hard charging, self-critical, sensitive to criticism, continually anxious, and likely to suppress their emotions. It's as though they're pots that are ready to boil over and always in a state of tension. They get overwhelmed with the responsibilities of life and at times just want to disassociate themselves from everyone. They're easily blindsided by other people's actions and feel left in the dark about what's happening around them. They live with the fear of rejection and abandonment. They're perfectionists and believe they have to prove themselves so that they'll be needed and liked. They're easily frustrated and get angry almost to the point of rage when anyone expects them to do something without giving them the information or tools needed to make it happen. They dislike others telling them what to do or how to do it or bossing them around.

Associated emotions: Anger, rage, resentment, frustration, disdain, disgust, dread, shame

The needs behind the illness: Soul—to grow and express ourselves; mind—to feel secure and in control of our lives

What to change: Attitudes and thoughts

Multiple Sclerosis (MS)

General description: This is the breakdown of the myelin sheathing that protects the nerves. It becomes inflamed and begins to fail, short-circuiting the electrical flow, thus causing nerve inflammation. Repeated bouts of this irritation produce sclerosis (scarring), and although the sheathing can normally repair itself, the damage happens too quickly and the healing process isn't able to take place. It's a degenerative disease of the central nervous system that can progress slowly and may even disappear for periods of time and then recur. It's an autoimmune disorder and appears to be connected to the herpes zoster virus and Epstein-Barr.

Psychological implications: The common implication is sufferers' inability to trust themselves, their intuition, or the process of life—that they will have what they need to survive. There's a tendency to feel out of control so they try to overschedule and overplan. They're strong-minded, opinionated, and rigid in their thinking and believe that they're always right and everyone else is wrong. They're resistant to change until they fully understand what it entails and how it will affect them. They display obsessive-compulsive behavior. They feel that they alone are responsible for solving everyone's problems; yet when asked for help, they become resentful and feel that others are taking advantage of their good nature. They tend to overanalyze situations and problems. As a result, they become mentally immobilized and indecisive and are afraid to do anything for fear of doing something wrong. They'd rather stay where they are and avoid decisions than make a mistake they'll regret later. Analysis paralysis is a common problem for them.

Associated emotions: Anxiety, anger, sadness, disgust, dread, terror, fear of the unknown, fear around survival, fear of betrayal

The needs behind the illness: Mind—to feel secure and in control of our lives

What to change: Thoughts

Plantar Fasciitis

General description: This is the most common cause of foot and heel pain. It's a chronic inflammation problem caused when the plantar ligament is injured or hyperextended. Since the plantar fascia has no elastic properties, repetitive stretching causes microtears to form, which then become inflamed. As the tight fascia is pulled, calcium is deposited in the microtears. If it isn't dealt with, meaning the plantar ligament isn't stabilized and protected, these calcium deposits build up and cause bone spurs. This condition is common in those who are on their feet a lot, dance, regularly use treadmills, and run.

Psychological implications: There are two differing messages behind plantar fasciitis. The first has to do with these people feeling stuck and being afraid to move forward. Part of the problem is that they feel they don't have the support they need, yet they don't ask for it. Much of their behavior is driven by what's urgent rather than what's important, which builds deep-seated resentment. They have difficulty getting closure and tying up loose ends. They suffer from the fear of the unknown and, as a result, feel frozen in their tracks. They're confused about who they are and what action needs to be taken in order to make things happen. They don't feel rooted in reality and are out of step with the world. They live in their heads and have difficulty being present in the moment.

The second message has to do with their tendency for discontentment and dissatisfaction. As a result, they over-extend themselves and push to do and accomplish more. They're afraid of staying in one place too long for fear that life will pass them by. They're relentless in the pursuit of their goals and run from one thing to another. Their perspective is that if a little is good, then a lot is better.

Associated emotions: Resentment, frustration, anxiety, irritability, disgust

The needs behind the illness: Mind—to feel secure and in control of our lives

What to change: Thoughts

Prostate

General description: The prostate is a walnut-size gland that produces the essential fluid to carry sperm. It also controls the volume of the flow of urine from the bladder, and while most men won't discuss their concerns about prostate problems, they weigh heavily on their minds because they're the male equivalent of breast cancer. There are basically three kinds of prostate issues:

1. Enlargement of the prostate, called benign prostatic hyperplasia (BPH)

2. Prostatitis, a bacterial infection

3. Prostate cancer

Psychological implications: These men see themselves as being self-contained, meaning they believe that they don't need to rely on others. They have difficulty sharing their emotions because they see doing so as a sign of weakness. There's shame about not living up to other people's expectations or not being responsible; they believe that they've somehow failed at fulfilling their role as a provider and protector. There's a sense of letting down those they love, which can express itself in impotence. There are buried emotions of anger, guilt, and grief as the result of divorce, job loss, or poor health. They see themselves as being ineffective, powerless, and having outlived their usefulness. Many times prostate issues in later years are the result of being thrust into a strong masculine role early in life by mothers who pushed them to suppress their emotions and act like men they could be proud of. The maternal expectations didn't allow them to learn how to express themselves in a healthy way. Relationships with controlling and domineering fathers can also inhibit their ability to develop the positive expressions of emotions.

Associated emotions: Shame, guilt, grief, sadness, sorrow, disappointment, anger, indifference

The needs behind the illness: Soul—to grow and express ourselves; body—to connect with other people and feel loved

What to change: Attitudes and patterns

Rheumatoid Arthritis (RA)

General description: This is an autoimmune disorder in which the immune system misidentifies a part of the body, such as the collagen in the connective tissue in a joint, as an enemy and attacks it. The collagen breaks down and is replaced with scar tissue, making the joint stiff or frozen. Contributors can include genetics, viral and bacterial infections, food allergies, chronic inflammation, adrenal exhaustion, and prolonged use of aspirin and cortisone.

Psychological implications: For those with RA, a primary emotional contributor to the condition is discontentment—with life, themselves, their relationships, their bodies, and their health. They see life as difficult and feel torn apart by the conflict between the needs of other people and themselves. There's a tendency for passive-aggressive behavior. Depression is common, as are feelings of being emotionally vulnerable. Their lives are plagued with inner turmoil, in a state of emotional upheaval, fraught with long-term tension, and never what they expect. They perceive themselves as stuck and unable to move forward, which is the fault of other people, circumstances, or bad luck that keeps them where they are. They become irritated with themselves and turn on themselves in their self-talk. They suffer from chronic anger and resentment. Rather than discussing the issues responsible for these emotions, they bury them, rationalizing that it's better to keep quiet than to create a problem.

Associated emotions: Anger, bitterness, resentment, guilt, disgust, anxiety

The needs behind the illness: Soul—to grow and express ourselves

What to change: Attitudes

Sciatica

General description: Sciatica is a common form of lower-back pain that radiates along one of the two sciatic nerves, each of which goes down the back of the thigh, calf, and into the foot. In the ankle it breaks off into two branches, one following the inside of the foot into the big toe, and the other running outside the foot and into the little toe. Most cases of sciatica occur when one of the spinal disks swells, ruptures, herniates, or bulges out, exerting painful pressure on the sciatic nerve. It can also be caused by tight muscles and prolonged sitting and leaning back in a chair.

Psychological implications: These individuals have difficulty integrating their physical selves with their spiritual selves. Consequently, they feel pulled apart and immobilized. The metaphor of sciatica is being frozen with fear around manifestation. Significant contributors to the condition are struggles with time and money and the fear of survival. They feel as though they're carrying the weight of the world on their backs because they have no one to help bear the load or support them. There's deep-seated resentment, survival anxiety, loss of direction, and avoidance of doing what they know they need to do. They're hypercritical, overburdened, overwhelmed, overextended, and overly independent. They don't ask for help or want it, but they're disgusted when no one assists them. They're angry with themselves because they're in a situation they can't change and disappointed in themselves because they won't stand up and confront the situation.

Associated emotions: Resentment, frustration, anger, disappointment, indignation, loneliness

The needs behind the illness: Soul—the need to grow and express ourselves

What to change: Attitudes

Shingles

General description: This is a herpes zoster virus from the same family as the one responsible for chicken pox. Shingles are skin eruptions of acute, inflammatory, hypersensitive, painful blisters that surface on the trunk of the body along a peripheral nerve. It's an acute nervous system infection. When the virus is active, it can cause a low-grade fever, muscle aches, and intense pain in the area of the body affected.

Psychological implications: These individuals have a core theme that things are never right. As a result, they live with chronic frustration and disappointment. They easily become agitated and irritated when things don't go the way they want. They tend to micromanage tasks, people, and life for fear that everything will fall apart. They experience rage over the loss of support and money. They're anxious and nervous about life and relationships. They feel that others take advantage of their good nature and suck them dry of energy. They focus so much on their physical needs that they feel unplugged from their spiritual nature. When overwhelmed, they'll isolate themselves, avoid interaction, and wallow in their own self-pity. They'll turn on themselves when they don't meet their own expectations. They become judgmental and self-critical to the point of creating self-destructive behavior. They're desperate to prove that they can succeed and manifest their dreams—and that they can do it without the help of anyone else, which is a real dichotomy because they expect others to be there to help and support them.

Associated emotions: Disappointment, anger, frustration, shame, guilt, worry

The needs behind the illness: Body—to connect with other people and to feel loved

What to change: Patterns

Stroke

General description: A stroke is a blockage of the blood supply to the brain that causes the brain cells to die wherever the stoppage occurs. Contributors can be irregular heartbeats, high blood pressure, diabetes, high cholesterol, obesity, smoking, excessive amounts of salt, and stress. Men tend to be more susceptible to strokes than women.

Psychological implications: These people worry, fret, and have trust issues. They tend to be aggressive, domineering, confrontational, and relentless in their need for control. They have explosive tempers and focus on problems rather than solutions. They become frustrated with those who say they'll do something but don't follow through. Consequently, they have difficulty delegating. They're compulsive overachievers, yet resent having to carry the burden of responsibility for anyone else. They're either feeling on top of the world or down in the dumps, which means extreme emotional highs and lows. When hitting bottom, they become consumed with negative thoughts that clog the brain and distort how they see the outer world. They feel that it's unsafe and try to isolate themselves as a means of protection. They're prone to depression and have a difficult time dealing with change. They need to have power over their environment and are aggressive in the pursuit of that control. They're secretive and suppress their feelings because they're worried about being vulnerable. Other fears associated with stroke are that of the unknown, survival, and betrayal.

Associated emotions: Anger, rage, frustration, resentment, hostility, dread

The needs behind the illness: Mind—to feel secure and in control of our lives

What to change: Thoughts

Thyroid Problems, Low Thyroid Functioning

General description: Hypothyroidism means an underactive thyroid where the gland ceases to produce adequate thyroid hormone to meet the body's demands. As a result, metabolism slows down. Hashimoto's disease is the most common cause of an underactive thyroid gland and the most common cause of a goiter, an enlarged thyroid.

Psychological implications: These individuals are afraid to speak up for themselves and express their needs. They suffer from feelings of inadequacy and have the perception that everyone can be successful except them because things are never right—it's never the right time or place. They tend to wallow in self-pity and have a difficult time pulling themselves up from the doldrums of life. They see success as something that always eludes them no matter how hard they try. They feel as though they're always out of step with the world, and they never seem to fit. There's a tendency to suppress their emotions and have almost a secretive side to their personality. Their metaphor is: "I share how I feel, but nobody listens." They're deeply resentful that no one hears them or cares. They feel alone and unsupported. They suffer from low self-esteem and struggle with getting people to accept them. They want to win the respect of others but tend to undermine themselves by playing small.

Associated emotions: Sadness, sorrow, despair, frustration, loneliness, despondency

The needs behind the illness: Soul—to grow and express ourselves

What to change: Attitudes

Tinnitus

General description: Tinnitus is an inner ear problem where there's an internal sound. It can be a ringing, whistling, chirping, clicking, or hissing. It can be constant or intermittent, loud or soft; and it's distracting, irritating, and annoying.

Psychological implications: "Is anybody listening?" and "Don't tell me what to do" are the two most common metaphors for tinnitus. These people feel like something inside is trying to send a message, but the content can't be heard. On the other hand, they don't want to listen to anyone else's rhetoric. They'd rather march to their own drummer. There's no compliance with rules for them, and there's a tendency to keep mentally rehashing and replaying a conversation that hurt them emotionally. They can be stubborn and refuse to listen to what others have to say. They also don't listen to their inner voice.

Associated emotions: Disappointment, resentment, grief, frustration, displeasure, anger

The needs of the illness: Soul—to grow and express ourselves

What to change: Attitudes

Only You Can Heal Yourself

The fundamental principle of psychospiritual healing is change, but not necessarily shifting everything at one time or tackling something so ominous that you'll procrastinate in taking the necessary steps. It's about making one simple modification at a time, such as altering a thought, an attitude, or a pattern of behavior. In doing so, you'll attract what you want. You'll live the life you desire and experience the good health that will make it possible for you to enjoy the pleasures available.

However, I feel that I should offer this warning: Once you begin the process of change, your life will never be the same. You'll find other people asking what has happened to you. They may become uncomfortable because they can no longer control you or guilt you into your old patterns. You might even find some individuals wanting you to share your newfound wisdom and disclose the steps you took to heal yourself.

What are those steps? You'll find them in the final chapter.

CHAPTER 13

Steps for Healing Yourself

As I've presented you with the knowledge and awareness of illness in the body, I have these hopes for you:

- Your perception of illness has sufficiently shifted so that you realize it isn't just the result of one factor, but of many.

- You're aware that healing is a personal journey and not a one-size-fits-all treatment plan, only you can heal yourself, and everyone else is merely there to support the process.

- You've recognized that healing requires removing the hidden contributors behind illness on all levels—mental, emotional, physical, and spiritual—and that it isn't about suffering, nor does it have to be stress filled.

- You understand that all healing requires is knowing what steps to take and where to begin the process.

- You know that you must provide your soul, mind, and body with what they need.

- Most important, you believe that healing happens *only* when there's change.

Step 1: Change Your Thoughts

The first step in the healing process begins with changing of thoughts. Why here? Your thoughts are responsible for the condition of your mental state and determine health or illness. They define who you are, what you think, how you act, and what you become. The power of a single thought changes everything about you, and does so instantly. It alters the chemistry in the brain and body, the flow of energy in the energy body, how you feel about yourself, and whether your soul finds its physical expression through your words and actions.

When you think negative thoughts, you're sending illness messages throughout your body to every cell. You're impeding the physical ability to function properly and breaking down your immunity. The result is that your cells become vulnerable to viruses and infections and lose their ability to remain healthy and viable. The bottom line is that you're creating an unhealthy mental state.

On the other hand, when you think positive thoughts, you're sending healthy messages that tell your soul, mind, and body that all is well. You're building your immunity and revitalizing cells, and you're creating the internal environment for good health. *Thoughts are associated with the needs of the mind, which is to feel secure and in control of our lives.*

Here are some things you can do that will help you change your thoughts:

- *Eavesdrop on your self-talk.* Pay attention to how you speak to yourself because it reflects the quality of your thoughts. When you hear yourself saying things you wouldn't tell your worst enemy, stop immediately.

- *Discover your inner guide and learn to listen to it.* This isn't your conscious mind, it's your intuition. How do you tell the difference? The former is what nags you and berates you for not doing something or not getting it right. It creates anxiety and stress. What you're listening for is the voice of your soul, and it never scolds you or creates anxiety. Instead, it encourages, inspires, offers possibilities, and creates excitement. It stimulates the need to change your thoughts. If you're accustomed to listening to and only acting on the rhetoric and demands of your conscious mind, this one may take some practice and concentration. However, the benefits for doing so are many.

- *Avoid becoming bored.* Boredom creates the mental environment for negative thoughts to bubble to the surface and replay their messages over and over again. When the brain becomes idle, it will do almost anything to fill the nonproductive thinking time. It will even create pain and illness if that's what it takes to stay busy.

- *Continue to learn.* Acquiring knowledge stimulates the development of neurons and encourages the brain to reorganize itself when it's stuck in unhealthy thinking patterns. It keeps the mind agile and the brain cells talking to each other. You can dust off the mental cobwebs by reading more, enrolling in college, or taking adult-education classes. Develop new skills that stretch you mentally and become an expert in something that interests you.

- *Express your creativity.* It's hard for the brain to become bored or focus on the negative when it's busy coming up with something new. Creativity feeds the mind and soul and brings your inherent talents and gifts to fruition. It moves your thoughts from what's familiar to what's new, and it creates a level of mental excitement. Learn to paint, play music, or write. Do anything that allows the right brain to express itself. Creativity allows you to express yourself in ways that conditioning doesn't, and it makes room in your life for fun.

- *If you can't eliminate it—reframe it.* Carl Jung said, "It all depends on how we look at things, and not on how they are in themselves." If you have trouble changing your thoughts, then revise their role. Rather than seeing them as limitations, view them as opportunities. Welcome them as you would a good friend and see them as a challenge that you're eager to meet. Ask yourself: *How can my thoughts best serve me in my healing process?*

• *Evaluate your choices before you make them.* Ask yourself: *Am I making this choice for my reasons or for someone else's?* Your answer will tell you if the decision is right or not. Pick options that are important to you and that support your values and principles. Don't compromise yourself or your integrity. Remember that personal satisfaction and feeling good about yourself are much more important than money in the bank or being liked for the wrong reasons.

• *Break out of your mental ruts.* If you're prone to sticking with what's tried-and-true, take a risk and attempt something different—think out of the box. In doing so, you'll clean out the old mental clutter that accumulates with repetitive thoughts and make room for exploration and creativity. Ask yourself: *What if?* and *Why not?* Drive home by a different route, develop new interests, invite curiosity back into your life, embrace the unexpected, and take pleasure in the surprises that the unknown offers.

• *Develop a holistic sense of reality.* Don't allow your fears, prejudices, and beliefs to limit your sense of reality. They shrink your outer world down to what's safe and secure and limit what you can achieve. Instead, expand your perception of reality so that you're able to see how your environment is affecting your inner world. Engage your intuition and use it as an observation skill, allowing you to see things for what they really are rather than what you want them to be. This will allow you to discover the opportunities life offers. It will also let you make better, healthier choices.

- *Seek solutions rather than dwelling on problems.* The purpose of life is to have experiences, and with them come problems—sometimes lots of them. What defines your health isn't the number of challenges you have, it's how you deal with them. See obstacles as the chance to exercise your mind and not as insufferable dilemmas. When you solve your own problems, you free yourself from others' control and their problems. You become the master of your own destiny and attract experiences that promote good health.

Step 2: Change Your Attitudes

Is the glass half empty or half full? How you answer that familiar question is an indicator of your attitude. The second step in the healing process is to change attitudes, because they determine how you emotionally engage in life and how you interact with other people. Attitudes impact the well-being of the body. They encompass all emotional expressions, both positive and negative, and are multidimensional in nature, meaning that you could have an upbeat spiritual outlook but a detrimental mental position.

Healing requires an affirmative disposition on all levels—spiritual, mental, and emotional. Attitudes influence your outlook on life, impact your self-image, affect your demeanor, and determine your willingness to participate in recovery. If positive, they manifest courage, hardiness, and resiliency—all qualities that are needed to endure the challenges life presents you. If negative, they limit, create fear, and distort your perception of what you're capable of achieving.

Attitudes reveal when you're feeling confident and when you're feeling like a victim, and they tell other people where you are long before you ever say a word. They affect your commitment to remain steadfast in your convictions, determining whether you'll waver under pressure. *Attitudes are associated with the needs of the soul, which is to grow and express ourselves.*

Here are some things you can do that will help you change your attitudes:

- *Develop an awareness of your needs.* This doesn't have to be an emotionally draining or complicated, time-consuming analysis. You can start on a small scale, such as recognizing that you need a few minutes of quiet when getting home from work before plunging into the demands of your family members, or that you need to be able to spend time with your friends without feeling guilty or worrying about how others feel. Allow yourself to put your needs first by doing things you enjoy.

- *Reframe your perceptions of emotions.* Emotions are healthy—they're the soul's way of telling you how you feel about something, and they alert you when you're compromising yourself. In the case of anger, the message is that whatever is causing it needs to change right now because it's putting you in an unhealthy situation. It reveals the degree of compromise you're feeling and tells you that your personal boundaries have been violated. When you realize that you're angry, find ways to express it so that it isn't destructive to you or the other person. Learn how to work through your wrath without compounding it with other emotions such as guilt, worry, or resentment.

- *Allow yourself time to cry if you need to.* At some point in time, we all need a good cry to release the emotions we bury inside. Weeping releases healing chemicals that are carried throughout the bloodstream to all parts of the body and is even known to expedite the healing of skin wounds. It also helps you be more effective in coping with the challenges of life.

- *Treat yourself with the same kindness you share with others.* It's an interesting aspect of human nature that we'll be kind to strangers and those we're fond of, but we have a difficult time showing ourselves the same care. Instead, we tend to berate ourselves for our perceived inadequacies and expect perfection—even when we try something for the first time. Lighten up on yourself and concentrate on the things you do well. Be patient and pat yourself on the back when you do something you feel good about.

- *Love.* This emotion is a powerful healer and an effective attitude adjuster. It makes it possible for you to see yourself through another person's eyes and understand just how loving, caring, and wonderful you really are. It's the reward of life and the gift that keeps on giving—the more you love, the more affection you receive in return. Dr. Bernie Siegel says it best: "If you love, you can never be a failure."

- *Practice self-forgiveness.* If you can believe that there aren't any mistakes or complete losses in life, only opportunities to learn, then practicing self-forgiveness is a much easier task. Accept yourself for who you are, including your frailties and imperfections. The gift of self-forgiveness reconnects the soul, mind, and body. It allows the energy of the heart to flow unrestricted throughout the physical self, carrying with it healing messages to every cell. Self-forgiveness is the ultimate expression of self-love.

- *Laugh more.* It's difficult (if not impossible) to maintain a negative attitude when you're having a good laugh. Besides, it's good for the body—a kind of internal exercise program— because laughter works your lungs, heart, brain, and muscles. Curl up with a humorous book, watch a funny movie, or go somewhere you can be around children. Notice how many times they laugh and what they find amusing. You might even discover yourself laughing at the simplest things. In his book *Anatomy of Melancholy*, written almost 400 years ago, Robert Burton said, "Humor purges the blood, making the body young and lively."

• *Develop a gratitude attitude.* Gratitude opens your heart and floods your body with the healing energy of love. It births only positive emotions and creates a sense of happiness because it helps you remember what's truly important in life. Being grateful encourages random acts of kindness and keeps you focused on what's right and good in your life. It helps you develop an appreciation for simple things and reminds you to give thanks for all you have. It adds elements of awe, wonder, pleasure, and even ecstasy to the mundane. Gratitude makes you feel good, promotes health, and benefits the soul.

• *Never give up hope.* Even when times are difficult and you feel that you're in the darkest night of your soul, don't give up hope, because where it exists, there's no fear. Hope can be more powerful in the healing process than any treatment offered by physicians. It gives you the strength to confront whatever life presents you and to do so with grace and confidence.

• *Keep a healing journal.* Nothing heals the emotional wounds of your past quicker than bringing them to the surface so that you can see them in the light of day. When old hurts and their strong emotional charges are held within the confines of the brain, they feed on themselves until they insidiously break down your ability to transmute them. They become bigger than life, create abnormal behavior, and distort your self-perception.

A healing journal allows you to put to words your fears, your hurts, your insecurities, and the things from the past that you wouldn't feel comfortable sharing with anyone. It takes what's inside out of the secret mode. Like the stroke of a mighty sword, the pen brings forth how you felt then and how you feel now. It allows you to see how those experiences have affected you and are still having an impact. At the same time, writing about them releases the associated emotional charges without your feeling vulnerable. The gift of journaling is that it motivates you to tackle an old hurt when you're ready and feeling emotionally strong.

Step 3: Change Your Patterns

The final part of the healing process is probably the easiest because all you have to do is step back and become an observer of your own behavior. You'll immediately see your habits, comfort zones, core themes, and personality idiosyncrasies and recognize the patterns they've created. However, starting here really isn't the answer. Sure, it relieves the pain and helps manage stress, but it doesn't heal what created the patterns in the first place. That's why it's so important to begin with Step 1 and find the source—the thought.

But discovering the single seed responsible for a pattern isn't necessarily easy. Over the years, it has been buried by other thoughts that the brain deemed similar. Here's where patterns can really be of value because they identify not only the one concept you're seeking, but also the quality of all of the thoughts behind the repeated behavior, allowing you to focus on what you need to change.

Think about a pattern that seems to limit you. Perhaps you're always late. This has become a major point of contention in your personal relationships or at work and has actually prevented you from getting a promotion. Yet as you observe this, you recognize that there are situations when you're not only on time, you're even early. What's the difference? What are the thoughts behind being late? Are they resentful because you have to do something you don't want to? What's behind being on time? Do these thoughts reflect what you want to do?

Once you recognize the difference, it's easy to alter the pattern by changing the thought. Instead of doing things for other people's reasons, do them for yours. *Patterns are associated with the needs of the body, which is to connect with other people and feel loved.*

Here are some things you can do that will help change your patterns:

- *Become aware of your patterns.* When you're aware of them, you can consciously choose those you want to keep and those you want to change.

- *Create a close circle of friends.* They keep you engaged in life and invite you to participate in new and different things. They create a safe place where you can share your emotions, fears, sorrows, innermost desires, dreams, and goals without fear of retribution. They expand your self-perception and will even let you know when something you're doing isn't right for you. It's difficult to remain healthy when you isolate yourself. Study after study shows that people who are in a long-term intimate relationship, who belong to clubs and organizations, and who have a strong circle of friends live longer, healthier lives.

- *Get involved and help others.* Nothing gets you out of the mental doldrums faster than reaching out to someone in need. The act of helping is actually wired into your brain. When you do things for others, it releases healing messages and endorphins. You weren't designed to be alone. You need people, and you need to be involved in life if you're to remain healthy. Join an organization whose cause is near and dear to your heart and volunteer time, money, or whatever resources you have to offer. The gift of helping others is that it bolsters you at the same time.

- *Try something new.* Branch out, even if it's just by trying a new recipe every week or changing the style or color of your hair. It's easy to get into ruts and take the path of least resistance when old patterns run your life. Do something daring such as ordering something unfamiliar off the menu or even going to a new restaurant rather than an old standby. Plan a different vacation than the one you usually take so that you can meet new people and engage in different social activities. Learn to dance, play music, or paint.

- *Put some play into every day.* Life becomes boring and dull if there's no play in it. Create discretionary time to do whatever you want and learn to savor leisure, even if your perception of fun is different from others. Recreation makes a huge difference in the body's ability to heal itself because it cancels out the stress and the negatives that come with the responsibility of being an adult. It's hard not to laugh and experience joy when you find yourself doing something that puts a smile in your heart. It's also more difficult to take life seriously when you're having fun.

- *March to your own drummer.* Rather than trying to look like or act like everyone else, find something that sets you apart from them, something that makes you unique. Build on that and use it as the inspiration to change old patterns. Surround yourself with people who are different and also march to their own drummer. Observe them and find what you admire about them. Perhaps they're visionaries, deep thinkers, artists, or activists. Being around those who believe in themselves can help you do the same.

- *Learn more about who you are.* Nothing changes patterns quicker than discovering something new about yourself. Study more about your personality and why you think and act the way you do. Engage in activities that reveal your natural talents and find out how to develop them. Let go of the thought that you can't teach an old dog new tricks. Everyone can learn if they use the right motivation. Get to know what motivates you.

- *Spend time in nature.* As an observer of the natural world, you'll begin to understand how your life also goes through cycles and that there are ebbs and flows. You'll discover how everything that exists in nature does so in a symbiotic way and how all is somehow connected, yet different. You'll observe the purity and simplicity of life and how each part of the environment doesn't attempt to be something other than what it is—it tries to be the best it can. You see that growth takes time, and that everything progresses at its own pace.

- *Keep on moving.* The value of movement is that everything is changing moment by moment. If you block motion, you block change, and like still water, you become stagnant. Without movement, there's no dance, work, or play. It keeps the energy flowing in the energy body and merges the inner and outer worlds. To move is to be alive; to inhibit action creates illness. Movement is good for the soul, mind, and body, and it breaks tired old patterns.

Illness as a Teacher

In its own unique way, illness is a great teacher. It brings to our attention to the fact that something caused it; and our job, if we want to heal, is to uncover and eliminate that cause. Our priorities immediately shift from the demands of the outer environment to the needs of our inner world. It helps us remember what's important and offers time for reflection and introspection. Being sick reminds us that we each hold within our very being a healing power that's so effective it can transmute cancer and other life-threatening conditions. Yet if we're to accomplish such a feat, illness reminds us, we must let go of the rhetoric that preoccupies us to the point that we forget to nurture the needs of the soul, mind, and body.

In his book *Head First: The Biology of Hope and the Healing Power of the Human Spirit,* Norman Cousins reminds us that "hope is the curative power of the soul and that an appreciation for life can be a prime tonic for what ails the body and the mind." When we're up to our elbows in alligators, it's difficult to remember that the objective is to drain the swamp. Illness acts as the catalyst that stops us in our tracks and immediately redirects our attention inward. This way we'll remember our life's objectives:

- Experience life joyfully.
- Love without fear of being hurt.
- Laugh often, play much.
- Learn from our experiences.
- Use what we learn to expand our self-perception.

- Free ourselves from the limitations of our conditioning.

- Grow personally and evolve spiritually.

- Live long and prosper from our lessons.

In many ways, illness makes it possible for us to reconnect with our souls and spiritual natures and link with our minds and bodies. At the same time, it offers us the opportunity to make the necessary course corrections that will get us back on track and help us remember who we are. Once we recall our true selves—versus what our conditioning tells us we should be—we're ready to move forward in life with a sense of confidence and the courage to change the thoughts, emotions, attitudes, beliefs, and core themes that are the root causes of our illnesses. Then we'll be able to create the lives and health we desire by healing ourselves.

I think Henry David Thoreau described the process of healing eloquently: "If one advances confidently in the direction of his dreams, and endeavors to live the life which he has imagined, he will meet with a success unexpected in common hours. He will put some things behind, will pass an invisible boundary; new, universal, and more liberal laws will begin to establish themselves around and within him; or the old laws will be expanded, and interpreted in his favor in a more liberal sense, and he will live with the license of a higher order of beings."

ACKNOWLEDGMENTS

Writing a book, any book, is the result of many hours of sitting at a computer hoping the words will flow freely and trying to capture on paper the love, support, and encouragement offered by the hundreds of people who are responsible for the soul of its message. This book is no different in the sense that it reflects not only the hearts of those who sat in front of me for a reading, but also their struggles with illness. They showed me what true grit was as many battled stage IV cancer, and how powerful hope was in the fight for their life. Many overcame their illnesses even when the physicians told them that they couldn't, and many transitioned into light. When I wanted to understand diabetes and its hidden meanings, they came; when I wanted to understand fibromyalgia and heart disease and their hidden meanings, they came. Each of them was my teacher, and all were responsible for the honing of my skills as a medical intuitive and for what I've shared in this book. I thank each and every one of you for making my life richer and for allowing me to touch the beauty of your light. The world is truly fortunate to have been blessed by your presence.

The book reflects the wisdom of the mentors in my life: Thoth, Hermes, Paracelsus, Hippocrates, Carl Jung, Sigmund Freud, Manly P. Hall, Edgar Cayce, and Louise Hay. It was through their writings that I came to understand that illness is the result of the mental state affecting the physical state and that there are many factors responsible for why we become ill.

It also reflects the interaction and validation of the many physicians who worked with me and sent me their patients when they weren't sure where to go next. It was great to be a part of your teams, and your openness to work with an intuitive speaks to your commitment and dedication to helping people heal. I know for many of you, your colleagues wondered what you were doing in speaking with an intuitive and probably questioned if you had lost your minds.

While bringing this book into manifestation has been a personal process, it wouldn't have happened if it wasn't for the urging and loving support of my husband, Bruce, who for 24 years has listened to me, helped me capture my research data, been by my side on the road and in the classroom, and spent many lonely nights while I sat at the computer writing books. His insight into my work, habits, and writing-style idiosyncrasies, and his ability to edit the work when frankly sometimes he wasn't even sure what I was trying to say is truly a gift in my life. It's rare to find a best friend, soul mate, and partner in the one you love. It's also rare to have a relationship and love that we would wish for everyone. Thank you for all you do.

Thank you to my girls, Diana and Cindy. You're always there for me and listen with loving and compassionate hearts. It's a joy to have you both working in the business. Each of you brings so much to the table and is so very talented. Diana, your business skills are a strong asset to the direction and future of the Ritberger Media Group and will help make my dreams come true. Cindy, you're a knowledgeable, gifted healer and help many people. We're a good healing team. Ashley, Grandma loves you dearly and marvels at your courage and joyful nature as you live with muscular dystrophy. You remind me every day how precious life is and how important it is to find pleasure in the simple things.

Mom, Dad, Ginger, and Petty, you all stood by me even in my darkest times of trying to figure out what to do with this altered way I see the world. Never once did you not believe me when I told you that I can see auras around people, plants, and pets. Sure there were those *Is she okay?* looks, but you loved me and have always been there for me. Thank you.

Shannon Littrell, editor extraordinaire, your mastery turns my work into something that's understandable and grammatically palatable. Not always an easy feat, but patient you are, as Master Jedi Yoda would say. I love your cheerful, helpful nature. It's a pleasure to work with you.

Jessica Kelley, you are a magician of words and content. After all is done, you make the book better by adding your special touch. Hay House is fortunate to have you on their team—as am I. Thank you for a job well done.

Thank you Louise Hay, Reid Tracy, Jill Kramer, Donna Abate, Margarete Nielsen, Carina Sammartino, and all of the Hay House gang for all you do for your authors. Thank you Summer McStravick, Diane Ray, Emily Manning, Joe Bartlett, Sonny Salinas, Kyle Rector, and Roberto Criado at **HayHouse Radio.com** for the great inspirational radio programs and for making doing a radio show fun. Hay House is such a bright light in a world where sometimes there is little.

Danny Levin you have always believed in me and encouraged me to do this book. I hope you enjoy it.

BIBLIOGRAPHY

Albertine, Ph.D., Kurt, *Anatomica,* New York, NY Barnes & Noble, 2001

Albrecht, Karl, *Brain Power,* Englewood Cliffs, NJ, Prentice-Hall, Inc., 1980

Alcamo, Ph.D., I. Edward, *Anatomy Coloring Workbook,* New York, NY Random House, 1997

Allen, James, *As a Man Thinketh,* Revell or the Peter Pauper Press, 1957

Berkow, M.D., Robert; Mark Beers, M.D., *Merck Manual,* Whitehouse Station, NJ, Merck Research Laboratories, 1997

Bradshaw, John, *Healing the Shame that Binds You,* Deerfield Beach, FL, Health Communications Inc., 1988

Brennan, Barbara Ann, *Hands of Light,* New York, NY, Bantam Books, 1987

Carter, Rita, *Mapping the Mind,* University of California Press, Berkeley, CA, 1998

Cooke, M. B., *Body Signs,* Queensville, Ontario, Canada, Marcus Books, 1982

Cousins, Norman, *Anatomy of an Illness,* New York, NY, Bantam Books, 1979

Covey, Stephen, *The 7 Habits of Highly Effective People,* New York, NY, Simon and Schuster, 1989

Dale, Cyndi, *New Chakra Healing,* St. Paul, MN, Llewellyn Publications, 2001

Damasio, Antonio, *Descartes' Error,* New York, NY, Putman and Sons, 1994

Doyle III, Bruce, *Before You Think Another Thought,* Charlottesville, VA, Hampton Roads Publishing Company, 1997

Epstein, Donald, *The 12 Stages of Healing,* San Rafael, CA, Amber-Allen Publishing, 1994

———, *Healing Myths, Healing Magic,* San Rafael, CA, Amber-Allen Publishing, 2000

Erikson, Erik, *Childhood and Society,* New York, NY, W.W. Norton, 1964

Fincher, Jack, *The Human Body,* New York, NY, Torstar Books, Inc., 1984

Freidman, H. S., ed., *Personality and Disease,* New York, NY, Wiley, 1990

———, *The Self-Healing Personality,* New York, NY, Henry Holt, 1991

———, *Hostility, Coping, and Health,* Washington, DC, American Psychological Association Press, 1992

Gallo, Fred, *Energy Psychology,* Boca Raton, FL, CRC Press, 1999

Goleman, Daniel, *Emotional Intelligence,* New York, NY, Bantam Books, 1995

Gray, Henry, *Gray's Anatomy,* New York, NY, Barnes & Noble Books, 1995

Hafen, Brent; Keith Karren; Kathryn J. Frandsen; N. Lee Smith, *Mind/Body Health,* Needham, MA, Allyn & Bacon, 1996

Hall, Manly, *Adventures in Understanding,* Los Angeles, CA, The Philosophical Research Society, 1969

———, *Man, Grand Symbol of the Mysteries: Thoughts in Occult Anatomy,* Los Angeles, CA, The Philosophical Research Society, 1972

Harman, Ph.D., Willis and Howard Rheingold, *Higher Creativity,* Los Angeles, CA, Jeremy Tarcher, Inc., 1984

Harris, Bill, *Thresholds of the Mind,* Beaverton, OR, Centerpointe Press, 2002

Hay, Louise L., *You Can Heal Your Life,* Carlsbad, CA, Hay House, Inc., 1984

Jacobi, Jolande, ed., *Paracelus,* Princeton, NJ, Princeton University Press, 1979

Jolly, M.D., Richard, *The Color Atlas of Human Anatomy,* New York, NY, Harmony Books, 1994

Judith, Anodea, *Eastern Body, Western Mind,* Berkeley, CA, Celestial Arts, 1996

Jung, Carl, *The Archetypes and the Collective Unconsciousness,* Princeton, NJ, Princeton University Press, 1959

———, *Psychological Types,* Princeton, NJ, Princeton University Press, 1971

Keleman, Stanley, *Emotional Anatomy,* Berkeley, CA, Center Press, 1985

———, *Patterns of Distress,* Berkeley, CA, Center Press, 1989

Kurtz, Ron, *Body-Centered Psychotherapy: The Hakomi Method,* Mendocino, CA, LifeRhythm, 1990

———, *The Body Reveals,* New York, NY, Harper & Row, 1976

Leadbeater, C. W., *Chakras,* Wheaton, IL, The Theosophical Publishing House, 1927

———, *Inner Life,* Wheaton, IL, The Theosophical Publishing House, 1978

Lewis, H. R., and M. E. Lewis, *Psychosomatics,* New York, NY, Viking Press, 1972

Lincoln, Ph.D., Michael, *Messages from the Body,* Redmond, WA, Talking Hearts, 1991

Lipton, Bruce, *The Biology of Complementary Medicine,* 2001

———, *The Biology of Belief,* Santa Rosa, CA, Mountain of Love/Elite Books, 2005

Lowen, M.D., Alexander, *The Language of the Body,* New York, NY, Collier Books, 1971

Luscher, Max, *The Four-Color Personality,* New York, NY, Simon & Schuster, 1977

———, *Personality Signs,* New York, NY, Simon & Schuster, 1981

Marieb, Ph.D., Elaine, *Essentials of Human Anatomy and Physiology,* San Francisco, CA, Benjamin/Cummings Science Publishing, 2000

Martin, Paul, *The Healing Mind,* New York, NY, Thomas Dunne Books, 1997

———, *Messengers to the Brain,* Washington, DC, National Geographic Society, 1984

McCracken, Thomas, *New Atlas of Human Anatomy,* Metro Books, 2000

Miller, Alice, *The Drama of the Gifted Child,* Translated by Ruth Ward, New York, NY, Harper Collins, 1981

Moyers, Bill, *Healing and the Mind,* New York, NY, Doubleday, 1994

Myss, Ph.D., Caroline and Norman Shealy, M.D., Ph.D., *The Creation of Health,* Walpole, NH, Stillpoint Publishing, 1993

Nelson, M.D., John, *Healing the Split,* New York, NY, State University of New York, 1994

Nuland, Sherwin B., *The Wisdom of the Body,* New York, NY, Alfred Knopf, 1997

Nunn, John, *Ancient Egyptian Medicine,* London, England, University of Oklahoma Press, 1996

Overbeck, Carla, *Systems of the Human Body,* Jonesboro, AR, ESP Productions

Ornstein, Robert and David Sobel, *The Healing Brain,* New York, NY, Simon & Schuster, 1987

Padus, Emrika, *The Complete Guide to Your Emotions & Your Health,* Pennsylvania, PA, Rodale Press, 1986

Page, Linda, *Healthy Healing,* Traditional Wisdom, Inc., 2003

Pearl, Dr. Eric, *The Reconnection,* Carlsbad, CA, Hay House, Inc., 2001

Pert, Ph.D., Candace, *Molecules of Emotion,* New York, NY, Scribner, 1997

Pearsall, Paul, *Super Immunity,* New York, NY, McGraw Hill, 1987

Ponder, Catherine, *The Dynamic Laws of Healing,* Camarillo, CA, DeVorss Publications, 1966

Rayner, Claire, *Atlas of the Body,* New York, NY, Rand McNally & Company, 1980

Restak, M.D., Richard, *The Brain,* New York, NY, Bantam Books, 1984

Ritberger, Ph.D., Carol, *Your Personality, Your Health,* Carlsbad, CA, Hay House, Inc., 1998

———, *What Color Is Your Personality?,* Carlsbad, CA, Hay House, Inc. 2000

———, *Love . . . What's Personality Got to Do With It?,* Carlsbad, CA, Hay House, Inc., 2006

———, Module Three, Science and Art of Intuitive Medicine, *The Effects of Emotions, Attitudes and Beliefs on Health,* Cameron Park, CA, The Ritberger Press, 2005

———, Module Four, Science and Art of Intuitive Medicine, *Hermetic Anatomy,* Cameron Park, CA, The Ritberger Press, 2006

Rogers, Carl, *On Becoming a Person,* Boston, MA, Houghton Mifflin Company, 1961

Rush, M., *Decoding the Secret Language of Your Body,* New York, NY, Simon & Schuster, 1994

Sternberg, M.D., Esther, *The Balance Within,* New York, NY, W.H. Freeman and Company, 2000

Targ, Russell and J. J. Hurtak, Ph.D., *The End of Suffering,* Charlottesville, VA, Hampton Roads Publishing Co., 2006

Trowbridge, M.Div., Bob, *The Hidden Meaning of Illness,* Virginia Beach, VA, A.R.E. Press, 1997

Weissman, Dr. Darren R., *The Power of Infinite Love & Gratitude,* Carlsbad, CA, Hay House, Inc., 2007

Whitmont, E. C., *The Alchemy of Healing,* Berkeley, CA, North Atlantic Books, 1994

Woodburn, Russell, *Essentials of Human Anatomy,* New York, NY, Oxford University Press, 1988

Wilber, Ken, *No Boundary: Eastern and Western Approaches to Personal Growth,* Boston, MA, Shambhala Publications, 1985

ABOUT THE AUTHOR

Carol Ritberger is a medical intuitive, a radio host, and an innovative leader in the fields of personality typology and intuitive medicine. She helps people understand how personality and emotional, psychological, and spiritual energy can lie at the root of illness, disease, and life crisis.

As the result of a near-death experience in 1981, Carol can literally see the human aura to identify where there are energy blockages that prevent the body from functioning properly. She has devoted more than 25 years to researching the impact of stress, emotions, and personality type on the health and well-being of the physical body. Her education includes personality behavioral psychology and behavioral medicine. She holds a doctorate in religious philosophy and a doctorate in esoteric philosophy and hermetic science.

Carol is the author of *What Color Is Your Personality?; Your Personality, Your Health; Love . . . What's Personality Got to Do With It?;* and *Managing People . . . What's Personality Got to Do With It?.* Her books have received national recognition for their innovative approach to self-help. She has a weekly live Internet radio show on **HayHouseRadio.com** and has appeared on national television and radio. Her work has been featured in publications such as *Good Housekeeping, Yoga Journal, Woman's World, Men's Health, GQ,* and *Healthy Living.*

Carol is the cofounder and executive director of The Ritberger Institute for Esoteric Studies, which offers personal- and professional-development programs. The goal of the institute is to assist its students in accessing and developing their intuition for business, personal, and spiritual growth. It offers an array of classes including personality training and certification and intuitive medicine training. Carol's personal goal is to influence the way allopathic medicine approaches the diagnostic and healing processes by bringing to it skilled and experienced intuitive diagnosticians and holistic practitioner professionals.

Carol lives in Northern California with her husband, Bruce, with whom she cofounded The Ritberger Institute.

For more information on programs and presentations offered through The Ritberger Institute, please visit her Website at **www.ritberger.com**.

Hay House Titles of Related Interest

THE AGE OF MIRACLES: Embracing the New Midlife,
by Marianne Williamson

*THE BODY "KNOWS": How to Tune In to Your Body
and Improve Your Health,* by Caroline Sutherland

*HELP ME TO HEAL: A Practical Guidebook
for Patients, Visitors, and Caregivers,*
by Bernie S. Siegel, M.D., and Yosaif August

PAST LIVES, PRESENT MIRACLES,
by Denise Linn (available March 2008)

RICHES WITHIN: Your Seven Secret Treasures,
by Dr. John F. Demartini (available March 2008)

*10 STEPS TO TAKE CHARGE OF YOUR EMOTIONAL LIFE:
Overcoming Anxiety, Distress, and Depression
Through Whole-Person Healing,* by Eve A. Wood

*THE WISDOM OF YOUR FACE: Change Your Life
with Chinese Face Reading!,* by Jean Haner

All of the above are available at your local bookstore,
or may be ordered by contacting Hay House (see next page).